BEYOND ORDINARY

The Secrets From *Jabez* To Unlock Your True Potential

ROBERT KREIS

ARK
house

Ark House Press
arkhousepress.com

Unless otherwise stated, all Scriptures are taken from the New International Translation (Holy Bible. Copyright© 1996, 2004, 2007, 2013 by Tyndale House Foundation. Used by permission of Tyndale House Publishers Inc., Carol Stream, Illinois 60188. All rights reserved.)

Some names and identifying details have been changed to protect the privacy of individuals.

Cataloguing in Publication Data:
Title: Beyond Ordinary
ISBN: 978-0-9756331-4-4 (pbk)
Subjects: [REL012120] RELIGION / Christian Living / Spiritual Growth; [REL077000] RELIGION / Faith; REL109000 [RELIGION] / Christian Ministry / General;

Cover design by NeueStudio | www.NeueStudio.com.au
Typeset by initiateagency.com

CONTENTS

PREFACE

Ordinary people do extraordinary things

His name was Jabez and 'Beyond Ordinary' is the story of his life and legacy.

I became aware of his story when it was popularized in this modern era by the now Dr Bruce H Wilkensen who wrote and released a book called, **"The Prayer of Jabez: Breaking Through to the Blessed Life"**[1] Released in the year 2000 it became a New York Times #1 bestseller, achieving in excess of 9 million copies sold in its first 2 years and is still popular and can be found in bookstores today along with study guides and other merchandise.

I purchased and read 'The Prayer of Jabez' in its early years and like many others, it introduced me to Jabez. Although I had read of his story previously, like many others, I had skipped over it without any great consideration. While my copy of Dr. Wilkensen's book was lost or given to another, I have revisited the account of Jabez life in some depth over the past years and found some great and inspiring life lessons that we all must embrace if we, like Jabez, want to live a life 'Beyond Ordinary'.

---

[1] Wilkinson, B., Kopp, D., & Dudash, C. M. (2000). The prayer of Jabez: breaking through to the blessed life. Sisters, Or., Multnomah.

If you stop and look around you. Listen to the stories of those you encounter everyday and you will find people, just like Jabez, who are inspiring because they have become more and done more than what life has said they could. Those individuals who in spite of their background or circumstance, having faced abuse or addiction, poverty, lack of education, serious illness or disability or any of the myriad of obstacles that life seems to have thrown at them to halt their progress and limit their potential, are exceeding all expectations. They are overcoming the determinism of fate that would condemn them to average or ordinary and for many, maybe much less than that, to become more than what life has declared they should be and often more than what they or others believed possible.

In every generation these individuals exist. Most will pass into history with little or no record of their life or achievements, yet they will have inspired and challenged those who knew them that more is possible. Some will have their fifteen minutes of fame, being honored by local or national authorities and receiving recognition through awards or accolades. Some will become known through books or movies that highlight their incredible achievements against the backdrop of their struggles and opposition. The select few will make it into the annals of history where they will live on down through the passage of time as an inspiration to the multitudes who follow. Their lives and accomplishments will be a testimony to all who hear their story that ordinary people can do extraordinary things.

You can settle for an ordinary life, but I believe that in the heart of every person, mine included, is the dream to be different and to make a difference, the deep desire of the soul to be more and to do more than what life has said is possible.

It is to that end I have sought to understand and apply some of the truths I have found in 'The Life and Legacy of Jabez' to encourage and hopefully inspire others and particularly you who are reading these words, to pursue a life 'BEYOND ORDINARY'.

The lessons he learned and the steps he took are not a magical formula nor a quick fix. They are life lessons, truths, that have to be birthed and sustained in the day to day realities of life. The deepest desires of the heart have to take form within the constant struggles and striving of life to achieve the possibility of what might be, the dream of what could be.

My aim is to inspire you to take one step beyond your current fears and doubts, to challenge yourself to attempt what you think you cannot do.

To all those who have taken a step beyond what they thought was possible, take the next step, and slowly day by day, step by step you will discover the power of this incredible truth: *"God, who by His mighty power at work within us is able to do far more than we would ever dare to ask or even dream of—infinitely beyond our highest prayers, desires, thoughts, or hopes."* (Ephesians 3:20 Living Bible (TLB))

The contents of my examination and exposition of Jabez's life are by no means exhaustive. Each aspect of the prayer is limited in its treatment and application. It is my hope and my prayer that you will not only read these chapters but also take time to meditate and seek further depths of meaning and application for your own life and that you, in turn, might use these truths to inspire and encourage others to seek to live their best life.

More is always possible and with this thought we are challenged to seek, to pursue and to embrace life 'BEYOND ORDINARY'.

INTRODUCTION

To dream and then to dare is to live 'Beyond Ordinary'.

There is little that lifts the human heart or inspires the human spirit to attempt more, to achieve more, to become more than the joy of achievement. That elation that comes by breaking the often sub-conscious barriers that we did what we thought we could never do.

One of the great joys in life is to see the person who, whether 16 or 60, attempt what they thought they could not do and while they may approach the task with fear and trepidation and they may stumble or even fail in their initial attempts, there is such pride and elation when you hear the words, 'I did it! 'I did it. I never thought I could, but I did it!'.

The greatest of human limitations is what we think
we cannot do and therefore never try.

To all those who have ever said, 'I can't do that' or thought 'I don't have ….." To those who think they are just average or ordinary and are therefore hesitant or reluctant to push the boundaries or to test the limits beyond what you already know. These pages are the lessons we learn from an ordinary man who with a less than favorable upbringing and against the odds became more and did more than what he or those around him thought possible.

He lived many many centuries ago. His story emerges from almost obscurity, hidden within genealogical records that recount the history of the tribes and families within the nation of Israel after the Babylonian captivity, circa 538 B.C.. The paradox is that his story exists within genealogical records yet his father is unknown, his mother is unnamed. There is no mention of a wife or children of his own and so we have this proverbial nobody appearing out of nowhere in a place he does not belong and yet out of this obscurity he emerges as a man of such renown that his name and his story is recorded in the annals of history in the greatest book ever written, that not just those who knew him but that each and every generation that follows might catch a glimpse of this man who dared to dream of a life beyond the dictates of his birth and circumstance and pursued the dream of what he might be.

'BEYOND ORDINARY' recounts the life and legacy of Jabez, a man who rose above the pain of his past and the less than favorable circumstances of his upbringing to become more honorable than his brethren.

This is the record of his life:

1 Chronicles 4:9-10
(transliterated from the Hebrew of the Masoretic Text)
"Now it came to pass, Jabez was honored more than his brethren and his mother called his name Jabez saying, 'because I brought forth in pain'. And Jabez called to Elohim (the God) of Israel saying, 'If only with blessing will You continue to bless me and will You greatly increase my territory and may it come to pass by Your hand with me that You will make me out from this evil without shaping me with the way of pain.' And to bring it into being Elohim (God) granted that which he asked for."

This account is like one of those summary biographs you would see on a plaque at a monument or in a museum describing the life of some notable person in a very succinct fashion. It gives you the barest of details yet provides a powerful portrait of a life that stood for something, that allowed them to stand out from the crowd and made their life worth remembering and recording for posterity.

The words of their story are meant to cause you to pause, to reflect and remember that in their example there are life lessons, character traits and values and perhaps even traditions that are worth holding onto and replicating if we want our own lives to mean something and contribute to the betterment of our generation and to history in general.

While we can never be them nor perhaps have any possibility of replicating what they did, we can be inspired to seek to make our own life count for something beyond our mere existence, as theirs did. We can be challenged by the possibility that we can live beyond any of the limits of our birth or upbring or the circumstances life may have imposed upon us.

They teach us that it is possible to rise above the injustices of the past, the intolerance of the present and the insecurities of an unpredictable future. To go beyond the determinism of those experiences we never desired nor deserved and to make our own mark on history's page. To rise above the fears, the frustrations and the failures that tell you: You can't! You won't! You shouldn't! You are just another ordinary person, one of the crowd. But nevertheless we are all possessed with the dream, that innate desire to be somebody and despite all that comes our way, all that seeks to belittle us and limit us, as long as the dream lives there remains the possibility that we might emerge through this journey of life to become the person we are capable of being and do things we never dreamed as possible. To this end we pursue a life 'Beyond ORDINARY'.

CHAPTER 1

NO ORDINARY LIFE

*The limitation of every human life
is what we think we cannot do
and therefore never try!*

From childhood, our parents, the people around us, life's circumstances both good and bad and the strength of our own personality define and dictate who we are. We are told what we can and cannot do. We are molded to become the product of our upbringing and environment with little self-determination.

Through our teenage years we reach the age of self determination. It is that stage of life where we tend to rebel against our parents and authority in general. Not because of a sudden urge to be rebellious but because we want and need to establish an identity beyond the boundaries that have defined us to this point. We want to be more than someone else's son or daughter. We need to be our own person. But to do that we have to create our own sense of identity, our own sense of purpose and destiny.

In this process, however, we often struggle. We become confused and frustrated because we do not know who we want to be and have little or no idea how to become this other person.

For many this struggle continues throughout life. We shape and reshape who we think we want to be or ought to be. We move in and out of relationships that mold us. We hone ourselves through further education and careers. Life itself carves deeply into our psyche and shapes us. But there still seems to be a very wide gulf between who we are and the person we want to become. There is a deep inner sense that somehow we were meant to be more and do more than what life has determined.

The question is: Do we accept life as it is dictated to us, as fate would have it, allowing it to define us and determine our course or is it possible to be transformed, to become this person we dream of becoming?

To begin to answer this question I want to introduce you to Jabez, a man, who despite the negative circumstances of his birth and upbringing was transformed to become more than who he and those around him ever thought possible.

His story is recorded in the Bible in :

1 Chronicles 4:9-10
(transliterated from the Hebrew of the Masoretic Text)
"Now it came to pass, Jabez was honored more than his brethren and his mother called his name Jabez saying, 'because I brought forth in pain'. And Jabez called to Elohim (the God) of Israel saying, 'If only with blessing will You continue to bless me and will You greatly increase my territory and may it come to pass <u>by</u> Your hand with me that You will make <u>me</u> out from this evil without shaping me with the way of pain.' And to bring it into being Elohim (God) <u>granted</u> that which he asked for."

Now, 1 Chronicles chapters 1 through 9 records the genealogy of the nation of Israel after their Exile. For the most part it is just a collection of names - tracing the ancestral lines of the tribes of Israel with their clans and families that existed before the Exile. These accounts are, in reality, just the record of generations of ordinary people living ordinary lives, being born, growing up, having families, surviving whatever life threw at them and then vanishing with little more than their names in a registry to show that they once existed.

This sequence is broken only by brief insights into the lives of a few of the more notable people, both good and bad, who somehow left their mark on history. In the middle of this list we find Jabez, one of these characters who stands out from the crowd. In these few lines, we have a very brief biography of an ordinary person, a man whose life was not defined by the circumstances of his birth nor by the pain experienced in his early years but inspired by a desire and determination to be more and do more than what life told him he could.

In his story we discover some truths that allowed him to make a mark on the pages of history, to be a person who did something beyond the ordinary and whose life is therefore worthy of recording as a pattern to inspire others, not just in his day but over the many centuries that have followed.

What is significant about Jabez is that he is remembered not for some outstanding achievement. He is renowned, not for having won a great battle nor for building a great empire, but for a simple prayer. Out of all the people in these nine chapters, he is honored above them all because of the prayer he prayed and the person he became when God answered his prayer.

As we step into the life of Jabez I want to be clear that our purpose is not to find some formula for success that will lead us to a quick fix for life's problems but to explore some truths that will prepare us and help us on the journey of discovery into finding the person we are capable of becoming and to put into play some of the principles that will enable us to live our best life.

This passage describes Jabez from two perspectives: First of all we see the person carved and shaped by the events that surrounded his birth and the harsh realities of his life that followed. Secondly, his prayer. His desperate cry to God for a different reality, for change. Change that would not just alter the circumstances of his life, but fundamentally determine the person he would become and the impact his life would have on those around him and those who would come after him.

Before we look at Jabez's prayer I want to look at the person, his character and see what we can learn from Jabez himself.

The first and standout lesson from the life of Jabez is:

You don't have to settle for an ordinary life

Jabez, above everything else, was a man who was not content to accept life or do life as it was handed to him.

Extraordinary things are not achieved by extraordinary people, but by ordinary people who refuse to settle for an ordinary life.

Human history is filled with ordinary people who, in spite of their personal circumstances, culture or environment, did extraordinary things. In every generation you will find countless examples of people who have achieved far more than they thought they could or ever would and changed communities, cities, cultures and left their mark in history.

Stop for a moment and look around you. Think about the people you know and you will find people, ordinary people, who in spite of their background and upbringing, in spite of what they have been told about who they are and what they could do, are exceeding all expectations, achieving more than what their circumstances and often the people around them and even what they, themselves, thought possible.

Think for a minute about the apostles, these followers of Jesus, a few simple fishermen, a tax collector, a political extremist, a dreamer. None of them, extraordinary. Living in an occupied country, with injustice, discrimination, unfair taxes, yet they changed the world. They took the message of Jesus Christ and presented it to their generation to the point where they changed their world and ours. Twelve ordinary men were credited with filling Jerusalem with their teaching (Acts 5:28) and of turning the world upside down in their own lifetime (Acts 17:6) and today around one third of the world's population profess to be christian because of these twelve ordinary men refused to be defined by their culture, their background, their life circumstances and dared to stand for something beyond themselves.

If I have a personal desire and passion it is to see people whom the world sees as average or ordinary, who perhaps see themselves as not really capable of anything special, rise to a level in life they never thought possible. People who discover and develop untapped reserves of potential and begin to live a life that challenges and changes some of the norms of our culture, that transforms the narrow thinking and narrow mindsets of some people who try to dictate and limit the potential of others because of their own fears and failures. I want to see people be more and do more than they ever dreamed possible because they come to know a:

Ephesians 3:20 Living Bible (TLB)
"God, who by His mighty power at work within us is able to do far more than we would ever dare to ask or even dream of—infinitely beyond our highest prayers, desires, thoughts, or hopes."

You do not have to settle for an ordinary life. You have the potential to be more and to do more than what you or others see as possible.

This is the message and the challenge of Jabez life.

So, what does it take to live beyond the dictates of life's circumstance? Beyond what you have been told you can be. Beyond what you have been taught you can or cannot do. What does it take to break away from the confines of the box life has put you in? To go beyond the limits that confine or condemn so many of us to ordinary when the lives of so many tell us it is possible for ordinary people to do extraordinary things. Things that make a real difference in our own life and the lives of those around us. Something that changes not only our own circumstances but influences and inspires others to do the same.

For Jabez this journey began with one simple step.

He prayed.

He prayed a prayer and God answered it. He became the person he thought he could never be and did things which seemed impossible because of a deep desire in his heart that he turned into a prayer. A prayer that God answered.

In the first instance, we might say, it was not what he prayed but simply that he prayed.

We do not know if this prayer of Jabez was his first priority or his last resort and in the end it is of little consequence. He prayed!

It is not a matter of whether he prayed in faith, out of fear or a deep sense of frustration and failure. He prayed!

The deep desire of his heart for change became his prayer and prayer is perhaps the greatest catalyst for change there has ever been. More lives have been changed throughout the course of human history by the simple act of praying than any of us will ever know.

If you want to go on the journey of living beyond the circumstances that are now dictating the course of your life then I would encourage you to do what Jabez did and that is to simply pray. It does not have to be an eloquent or detailed prayer. It just has to be a genuine cry from the heart for change. I have personally witnessed the transformation of many lives with the simple cry of: 'God, if You are really there, if You care, then please help me!'

Desperate people praying for the seemingly impossible seems to be a challenge that God delights in responding to.

"God granted that which he asked for."

Jabez prayed and God answered. That, my friends, is the recipe for no ordinary life. This bold prayer, Jabez's prayer says: I do not want to live an ordinary life. I do not want to live a life dictated by the pain and suffering of my circumstance. I want more than my name in the Registry of Births, Deaths and Marriages to show that I once existed. I may be an ordinary person but I do not want to live an ordinary life. I want to be seen. I want to be heard. I want to make a mark in history's page that will change the way that I and others that come after me will see life and do life.

This may seem impossible within the scope of what you can see or what you believe or even think is possible but it is not impossible with God.

1 Corinthians 2:9 New International Version (NIV)
"However, as it is written:
"What no eye has seen,
what no ear has heard,
and what no human mind has conceived"—
the things God has prepared for those who love Him"

God has a plan and it is not for you to live an ordinary life. His purpose for your life is —*infinitely beyond your highest prayers, desires, thoughts, or hopes.*

This prayer of Jabez encapsulates the cry of the human heart for change. The genuine cry of the human heart reaching out to God. It is the cry of hope, the uttered dream of an unseen reality, the possibility of what could be.

If the life of Jabez can inspire you to anything, let it be to search your heart and to find that dream which expresses the deepest desires of who you could be and what you could do and make it a prayer. A genuine cry to God for change, and specifically for that change that would instill in you the courage of your convictions and the confidence to pursue something that would make a real difference to you and inspire and challenge those around you to believe that both you and they have the potential to be more and do more than what life has said you can.

Remember this:

Extraordinary things are not accomplished by extraordinary people but by ordinary people who refuse to settle for an ordinary life.

Ephesians 3:20 Living Bible (TLB)
"Now glory be to God, who by His mighty power at work within us is able to do far more than we would ever dare to ask or even dream of— infinitely beyond our highest prayers, desires, thoughts, or hopes."

CHAPTER 2

LETTING GO

*"Letting go is to come to the realization that
some things are a part of your history,
but not a part of your destiny."*
Steve Maraboli

There are few who leave an indelible mark on the world. Most live lives that are dictated by their circumstances and therefore their destiny becomes one of fate rather than determination. Through its varied influences life will try to dictate and determine who you are and what you do. It will try to squeeze you and mold you into the shape that it dictates. But there comes a point, in truth many points during our lifetime, where through sheer frustration we think: 'There has to be more to life than this!'

I think Jabez was at one of these crossroads. Frustrated and fed-up with life as it was, he prayed a prayer that he hoped, against hope, would change the course of his life and it did when God answered his prayer.

But if change and pursuing our dreams and destiny were as simple as just praying a prayer we would all live out the life of our dreams. We would all be doing something significant and meaningful. But to get from where we are to where we want to be is not simple nor is it easy. There are real life challenges and changes that have to take place to become the person we dream of being and to achieve our sense of destiny.

The first of these challenges that Jabez and you and I have to face is dealing with the pain of the past.

Jabez's story, from birth through his childhood and into life as it now stood, was one marked by pain.

1 Chronicles 4:9-10:
(transliterated from the Hebrew of the Masoretic Text)
" *Jabez ... mother called his name Jabez saying,* *'because I brought forth in pain'.* *And Jabez called to Elohim (the God) of Israel saying, '... that You will make <u>me</u> out from this evil without shaping me with the way of pain.' "*

This aspect of the prayer is a play on words, in that the name 'Jabez' is derived from the word 'pain' and the latter part of the prayer is that the pain which had characterized his formative years would not shape or control his future.

We do not know exactly what this pain was but we are told that Jabez's mother experienced a trauma that affected her so deeply that out of her own pain she began to shape Jabez life from birth in a way that would characterize and to some degree control his early years.

I surmise that it was probably the death of Jabez's father just before his birth, whether through war, disease or some accident. Unlike all the previous genealogies Jabez' father is not mentioned. This and other aspects of the prayer including his mother's emotional state at his birth would lead to this being a reasonable conclusion. Besides the fact that her husband's sudden death would have been personally devastating it would also have left her destitute and very vulnerable. The emotional pain and grief coupled with the uncertainty about how she was going to provide for and raise this child greatly compounding the actual pain of giving birth. Whatever the scenario, pain characterized Jabez's early life.

Jabez, reaching a crisis point, begins to pray for change and the one aspect that pervades this whole prayer is that Jabez wanted a life different from the one that his circumstance had dictated to this point in time. To move forward, to embrace the future that he dreams of, Jabez had to break the hold of his past. He has to lay aside the burden that it was imposing on him if he was to embrace his best life.

All that is in your past, both good and bad, right and wrong, has brought you to the place where you are today and shaped the person you have become. But to change there must come a point where we realize that our history does not have to determine our destiny. Your past and its pain will either cripple you and confine you to a life within its limits or it will become the catalyst for change.

If the first lesson of Jabez is:

YOU DO NOT HAVE TO SETTLE FOR AN ORDINARY LIFE.

Then the second is:

YOUR PAST DOES NOT HAVE TO DICTATE YOUR FUTURE

As real and as raw as our past has been, if we are to move beyond our pain, we have to take a stand as Jabez did when he prayed this prayer and believe that change is possible. I have to believe that those things which have dictated and defined my life to this point will not be the things that determine my future.

Hebrews 12:1 New King James Version (NKJV)
*...Let us lay aside every weight, and the sin which so easily ensnares us,
and let us run with endurance the race that is set before us.*

'Run with endurance'. Endurance is the ability to go further than you think you can. It is the ability to go beyond the dictates of the pain of your circumstances and your present situation. When we run we hit a pain barrier, we get a stitch. We reach, as it were, the limit of our endurance. Your pain threshold will always try to dictate how far you can go and limit what you can do. Those with endurance learn how to break this pain barrier and go further than what their body, their mind and their circumstances say they can and this is the possibility that the life of Jabez portrays for us.

One of the things that limits our endurance is any weight we carry. Any serious runner seeks to limit the weight they carry, even down to the weight of their clothing and shoes. To become the person you are capable of being and to go as far in life as you possibly can, you need to let go and lose the weight your past is imposing on you.

No sane person would go into a race carrying a backpack full of rocks. Yet this is exactly how people try to do life when they refuse to deal with the issues of their past. How often have we said, or heard it said: 'That person is carrying a lot of baggage!' If you have ever carried a weight for a long time or over some distance, you will know it does not get lighter or easier with time. The longer you carry a weight the heavier it gets and the more you struggle with it.

Try this: Pick up a weight and then set yourself a goal, ie. carry it around for 15 minutes or walk a certain distance then let it go and try to achieve the same goal.

The lesson is this: the unresolved issues of your past may not stop you achieving everything you want in life but I can assure you of two things: 1)

It is easier to get to where you want to go without the weight and 2) You will go further, faster if you let it go.

This verse talks about sin literally as a weight that pulls us down and therefore keeps us from reaching our true purpose and full potential.

Jabez from the time of his birth had a weight imposed upon his life. A weight he was not responsible for but until he broke its power he could never truly move forward and embrace the fullness of who he could be and who he wanted to be.

The weight that many carry is often not the weight of their own sins, it is the weight of what has been imposed on them by the wrongdoing or sins of others. People do things and we carry the weight of the consequences of those actions, sometimes for our whole life.

So many people carry the weight of abuse: physical, emotional and sexual abuse. There are very few people, I would even dare to say none, who have not suffered unjustly at the hands of others. For some the severity of that abuse has had a more profound impact and the weight of guilt, shame or regret is a very heavy burden and becomes a limiting factor on their life.

Now, I don't want, in any way, to discount the seriousness or grievousness of your past or your pain. I don't know what you have suffered nor the pain you carry from it. But, I do know that as long as you carry it, it will hinder you and limit your capacity to be all you can be. While we may not choose the weight that is put upon us, we must come to the point where we assume the responsibility for breaking its power and letting go of the past because we recognize its ability to hinder and limit us and we realize the damage it is doing.

While I have never met a person who truly wants to live within the confines of their past, I have met many, an individual, who seems incapable of letting go and losing the weight their past is imposing on them and turning their life around to fully embrace who they were created to be.

So I have to ask: 'Why are we so incapable of letting go of our past when we so desperately want to move beyond it?'

To understand this we have to understand what it is we carry. What it is we are holding on to.

The weight we carry is often not just the physical or mental pain and anguish, nor even the shame and the guilt of the past, the thing we so often carry is a deep sense of injustice. Why me? It wasn't fair. I did not ask for this. I did not deserve this. They had no right to do that to me. And you are right. It was not fair. You did not deserve it. There is much in life we do not ask for and do not deserve.

Time can heal many wounds and some pain may dull with the passing of years but time cannot remove this deep sense of injustice. In fact, time and life experience often reinforce just how unfair, how unjust life really is. Wounds of anger, resentment and bitterness, even of regret and despair grow deeper not less with the passing of time. They are pain without ceasing. They become deep, open, festering wounds with no healing.

For us to be healed, for us to be whole, for us to be able to break the hold our past has over us and to let go of the burdens we carry, we need justice. But for justice to be served, for us to be free, there is a price to be paid.

There is a slogan that says:

No justice - no peace.

This slogan holds a powerful truth. Inherent within us is the feeling that someone has to pay for what has been done to me. Before we can have peace we must have justice. Before we can begin to heal, justice must be satisfied. Until someone has paid the price, until someone else has suffered, we can never have peace and we cannot heal.

Within the administration of Justice there are a number of truths we must learn.

The first factor is for us to realize that no amount of retribution or retaliation can ever make right any wrong you have suffered. The punishment of another does not undo the injustices of your past. You can never undo the wrong, the unfair or the injustice in life whether those things happen by your own doing or through someone else. You can go on punishing yourself or you can go on trying to punish everyone else but in the end you are still the one carrying the pain, the sorrow, the hurt. But when injustice is dealt with the right way, it allows you to let go and move forward and embrace a different future.

The second factor in dealing with our past is that we sometimes think that God does not care and that He does nothing about the injustice we have suffered and the pain we carry. But God never ignores sin nor overlook injustice. God fully recognises the wrongs and the injustices of life. He recognised that someone had to pay the price and God chose One to carry that burden, to pay that price. That someone is Jesus.

1 Peter 2:24 GOD'S WORD (GW)
Christ carried our sins in His body on the cross so that freed from our sins,
we could live a life that has God's approval. His wounds have healed you.

1 John 2:2 GOD'S WORD (GW)
He is the payment for our sins, and not only for our sins,
but also for the sins of the whole world.

I think that sometimes we think forgiveness is God expecting us to pretend like some things never happened, but that is not true. God does not ignore injustice He deals with it. The love that God has for you is so great, that He does not and cannot ignore your pain and suffering. He does not pretend that the injustice you have suffered is not real. He recognised it and paid the price for it.

What we have to realize is the cross does not make wrong, right. Jesus' sacrifice does not justify or condone sin. It is the price that is paid for all sin. Not just the sin you have committed but also that sin which all of the world and all of life has unjustly dumped on you. Jesus does not justify sin or wrong, He personally paid the price for it.

Isaiah 53:4-6 GOD'S WORD (GW)

He certainly has taken upon Himself our suffering
and carried our sorrows.
We thought that God had wounded Him,
beat Him, and punished Him.
But He was wounded for our rebellious acts.
He was crushed for our sins.
He was punished so that we could have peace
and we received healing from His wounds.
Each one of us has turned to go his own way,
and the Lord has laid all our sins on Him.

Jesus carried it so you don't have to, He was tormented, tortured, bruised and broken so you can be healed and whole and have peace. When you receive His forgiveness you are released from carrying the weight or burden of the consequences of what sin has imposed on you. Jesus carried it so you don't have to. Jesus suffered so your suffering could end. From this we can also forgive others. Your forgiveness does not release people from accountability, it simply means we hand over the responsibility of what happens to them to the One who does justly. We release ourselves from the weight of seeking either vengeance or justice. But, in doing that, forgiveness also releases me from carrying the weight of the consequences of their wrong, their sins in my life. When we have justice and forgiveness, we can have peace. When we realize the truth of the verse stated above, '*His wounds heal us.*'

When we are forgiven and learn to forgive others, God, through the price Jesus has paid on the cross, frees us from the penalty of sin and He also begins a process of healing and restoration so we can become the person we were born to be.

If you want to embrace your destiny you have to deal with your past. No amount of wishing it never happened or regretting it did happen or seeking revenge for what has happened will ever change certain realities. The reality is our past has marked us all. We all carry wounds and scars. Life has not and will not always be just or good or fair.

Things will happen that you did not ask for and that you do not deserve. Life will try to impose its burdens upon you and weigh you down with feelings of injustice, guilt, regret, anguish, bitterness and resentment until you can no longer move forward with such a load. You can carry it or you can recognise One has already carried it for you. Justice has been served and will be served but you need to let it go. You need to lay aside every weight that entangles you because if you don't it will keep you from the future you so desperately want.

The unresolved issues of your past will always limit your future until you, like Jabez, develop the courage and the ability to effectively break their hold on your life. Too many people carry the baggage of their past until it wears them out and they simply give up on the hopes and dreams of who they could be and what they were going to do. The heart of this prayer is not God change my past but God help me to let go of the weight it imposes on me so that those things that have determined my life to this point will not dictate my future.

When you are released from the burden of carrying the weight that your past seeks to impose upon you, you are free. Not just free from the impositions of the past but free to pursue the life you were meant to have. Free to become the person you were born to be.

Change is possible. You cannot change the past but you can make choices that will change your future. You can make decisions that will direct your life to a different end.

When Jabez prayed this prayer he was actively making those choices. He was changing his future and his destiny by refusing to allow his past to dictate that future.

YOUR HISTORY DOES NOT HAVE TO DETERMINE YOUR DESTINY

One of the highlights of Jabez's prayer is the seemingly impossible is possible.

God has a plan and it is not for you to live a life controlled by your past or your pain. To fulfill His purpose for your life:

Ephesians 3:20 Living Bible (TLB)
"God, who by His mighty power at work within us is able to do far more than we would ever dare to ask or even dream of—infinitely beyond our highest prayers, desires, thoughts, or hopes."

CHAPTER 3

POST A DIFFERENT SELFIE

The longer you live in the past,
the less of your future you have to enjoy

"*Sticks and stones may break my bones but names will never hurt me.*" While this rhyme is intended to build resilience against bullying and threats of violence, it is hard to think of a saying that is more blatantly untrue than this one. Name calling is perhaps the oldest and one of the cruelest forms of bullying and humiliation known to man. Names are powerful. Names are the primary source of our identity and as such our true name as well as other names or labels we are given carry a significant influence in shaping how we see ourselves - our self-image.

1 Chronicles 4:9b:
(transliterated from the Hebrew of the Masoretic Text)
"*... And his mother called his name Jabez saying,*
'because I brought forth in pain'."

The name Jabez is derived from the Hebrew word for 'pain'. It is actually the Hebrew letters for pain mixed up in a way that makes no real sense.

It is like Jabez' mother was expressing she could not make any sense of or understand what she had done to deserve the pain she was experiencing. There may be reasons why we experience some of the pain we do, but we often look at ourselves and think, 'What have I done to deserve this?' And generally speaking there may be no obvious reason why some of the pain or tragedies that befalls us have happened.

It is as if, even in the naming of Jabez, his mother was trying to say that everything in her life was mixed up and messed up and resulted in her pain. So when Jabez' mother named him, she projected onto him something of the mixed up, messed up, pain of her life at the time of his birth.

Now I have no idea why a mother would project such an image onto her child but she did.

Psalm 127:3 New Living Translation (NLT)
"Children are a gift from the Lord;
They are a reward from Him."

Jabez's mother could have identified him as a gift from God, a blessing or reward from heaven, instead she allowed her pain to rule her emotions and she projected onto this baby boy a horrible sense of identity and a projected destiny he did not deserve.

The mark of Jabez's life was 'pain'. The word for 'pain' comes from a Hebrew word meaning 'to carve'. (**'âtsab,**; a primitive root; properly, to carve, i.e. fabricate or fashion)[2] Professor James Strong gives this definition: "To carve an idol (as fashioned); also pain (bodily or mental)"[3].

An idol is an image that is shaped by carving. For Jabez and for many of us it means that there are experiences of pain through the trauma of loss,

---

[2]   https://www.blueletterbible.org/lexicon/h6087/kjv/wlc/0-1/
[3]   https://www.blueletterbible.org/lexicon/h6090/kjv/wlc/0-1/

sorrow, hurt and grief that carve and shape us and give us an image of who we are.

This word is also used with a negative connotation of an idol which also means that the image formed by this carving is a false image. When your life is carved and your self-image is shaped as a result of hurt, suffering and pain it is not the image that God created you to have. Life, if allowed to carve its own image of you will always give you a false image of who you are and what you can do. This was Jabez's experience. This was Jabez's life.

In the first instance, the name 'Jabez' means: 'He is the bringer of pain.' Almost like we would say to someone: 'You are bad luck.' Whenever you're around bad things happen. Jabez, you bring pain. You cause suffering and hurt. This was Jabez's identity.

But Jabez's name inferred much more than that. Within the Biblical and cultural context pain in childbirth was part of the original curse.

Genesis 3:16 New International Version (NIV)
"To the woman He (God) said,
'I will make your pains in childbearing very severe;
with painful labor you will give birth to children.' "

Because the pain that Jabez brought was associated with his birth, he was not just the bringer of pain, he was by inference the bringer of the curse. There was perhaps no worse label you could put on someone who was an Israelite than to say: 'You are cursed'. 'You are the bringer of the curse'. As an Israelite, you either lived under the covenant promises and protection of God and were blessed or you lived outside of it and were considered to be under the curse.

So, in naming Jabez, his mother implanted in him the idea that they were forsaken and uncared for by their God, and as a result of that, not only was he cursed and bound to a life of pain, but, through his existence he would bring that pain and that curse upon others. Within his own life, within his family and perhaps his village, Jabez would be seen as the cause of their problems and their pain. He was burdened with a life of almost unbearable guilt and shame, for things he had never done and had no control over.

His name projected on him an identity, an image of who he was and not only that but an image of who he was in the eyes of others and even more importantly an image of who he was in relation to God. Like Jabez, the image we have of ourselves will dictate a large portion of what we believe about ourselves, how we think others see us, and our perception on how we believe God sees us. We become who we are and often act the way we do in response to those perceptions, whether they are true or not.

This was Jabez's identity from birth. Every single time his name was called he was reminded that he was the cause of pain, the bringer of the curse, even though he himself had done nothing wrong. He gained his name and this identity simply by being born.

Many of us have suffered the rejection that comes from carrying a label not of our own choosing. People out of cruelty, fear or insecurity have projected onto your life and mine an identity and a future that you were never created for and never meant to carry.

But for Jabez there was one of those 'AHA' moments, whether a sudden revelation or a slow realization that dawns after years of deep, dark reflection. However it happened, for Jabez there came this moment of realization that who he was and who he could be were two entirely different people. Where life had placed him and what God had purposed for him were poles apart. They were diametrically opposed. It was from this realization that his prayer was born and his transformation begins.

You are and you can be more than the labels artificially attached to your life.

The person he was had been formed and shaped by the negative labels and perceptions of those around him, but God through His word, declared something completely different over Jabez life.

Whatever else happened and whatever other understanding Jabez came to, his prayer tells us that he began to understand that he was an Israelite, part of God's chosen people. He was invited to live in a covenant relationship with God and if he chose to do so he could be blessed and become a blessing. This was the covenant God made with Abraham, the father of the nation of Israel.

Genesis 12:2-3 New International Version (NIV)
"I will make you into a great nation,
and I will bless you;
I will make your name great,
and you will be a blessing.
I will bless those who bless you,
and whoever curses you I will curse;
and all peoples on earth
will be blessed through you."

This began to change the way Jabez saw himself and viewed his life.

Romans 12:2 J.B. Phillips New Testament (PHILLIPS)
"Don't let the world around you squeeze you into its own mold,
but let God re-mold your minds from within, so that you may
prove in practice that the plan of God for you is good."

This verse is very clear and very powerful if we can understand it. The world, circumstances, people, expectation and your personal belief systems will try to shape you in a way that is contrary to God's plans and purpose for your life. When that happens, as it does to varying degrees in all people, we need to come back to the One who created us, the One who saw us in our mothers womb and shaped us before anyone else saw us, before anyone else got their hands on us and began to shape us contrary to the original form for which we were intended.

Life will try to squeeze you into a mold, a shape that is of its own making, but God is saying, 'I made you different, you were not made to be squeezed into someone else's mold'. God does not squeeze you into some preconceived shape or form. He created you and allows you through this process of transformation to emerge into the person you were meant to be.

Life carves us from without
God transforms us from within.

The word 'transformed' is *metamorphoō* to change into another form, to transform, to transfigure. It is the word that we translate 'metamorphosis', the process by which a caterpillar transforms to become a butterfly.

God is not just trying to give you a new shape, or a different appearance, in hope that people and life will treat you better. He is wanting to create within you a new belief system and a new thought process, so you can see yourself as He sees you and think about yourself as He thinks about you and then out of that, act in a way that allows you to be seen as the person you were always meant to be.

Jabez through this prayer began to imagine or re-image himself according to how God saw him and who he wanted to be and not according to the perceptions nor the predictions of others. He began to see that the things spoken over him and about him were only some people's perspective or opinion. It was one side of the coin so to speak. But there was another perspective, God's perspective. Jabez began to realize he could have a life built around the promises and the truths that God declares over His life. He could begin to reshape and reimage himself according to who he was created and called to be. He could live a different life than the one that had been declared over him.

God will help you redesign your thinking, your understanding of who you are and from that process you will not be forced into some mold, you will blossom more like a flower. Through the process of nurture and time there will come an increasing unfolding and revealing of all that is within you. An unfolding revelation of that which is growing and developing within will be revealed with its own unique and inherent strength, potential and beauty for all to see.

There was this person who was the product of what his parent's and his peer's had decided and declared him to be but there was deep within Jabez heart as there is within the heart of every person the hope and the belief that we are more and can be more than what others see in us or believe about us.

This is because within every person, beneath what is seen, beneath what is spoken is the image that every person was created with and is meant to carry, that image is the image of God.

Genesis 1:26-28 New International Version (NIV)
"Then God said, 'Let Us make mankind in Our image, in Our likeness, ...'
So God created mankind in His own image,
in the image of God He created them;
male and female He created them."

To live a blessed life, you need to discover and begin to be transformed into the image you were always intended to carry and reflect, the image of God. To become all you can be you need to reshape or re-image your life according to the original plan and pattern of the One who created you and called you into being not after the one that has been carved into you by the hurt, pain and insecurities of others.

To do this is not a quick fix. It takes more than a quick prayer or a new mantra. It is a process of continually exchanging one level of thinking for another. From seeing yourself one way to continually and progressively discovering and seeing who you were created to be and who you can be.

The reshaping of Jabez's life was not the work of a moment in time. It began with the understanding of who he was and who he was not. An understanding of who he could be and who he was meant to be. So he began to pray, *'If only with blessing will You continue to bless me and will You greatly increase my territory and may it come to pass by Your hand with me that You will make me out from this evil without shaping me with the way of pain.'*

These aspects of this prayer hold within them the revelation of Jabez 'understanding of God's ability to transform a life. So that he became more honorable than all his peers because God granted him that which he requested.

God will not always remove you immediately from the horrific circumstances of your life. Don't ask me why, I don't know. What I do know is He walks in the fire with you (Daniel 3) and when you emerge you will not be burned and you will not smell of smoke and ash. The residue of where you have been and what you have endured and what has been forced upon you will not be what clings to you. As you emerge you will have a new image. You will be a different person. It will be like, that was another person, it was not the true me, the real me. The image you have will be the true image, the image of God, the way God sees you. The way God thinks about you. The person you can be and were meant to be.

When you break the power of your past you begin to empower a new destiny
When you break the power of projection you begin to embrace a new identity.

This prayer may have been prayed in a moment of crisis, in a time of anguish and despair but its story is not the story of a moment, this is the story of a lifetime discovering more and more who he was created and called to be. It is the unfolding of the purpose and potential that God has invested in each and every one of his creatures that when released allows us to understand the love of God that surpasses all understanding and that it is:

Ephesians 3:20 Living Bible (TLB)
"God, who by His mighty power at work within us is able to do far more than we would ever dare to ask or even dream of—infinitely beyond our highest prayers, desires, thoughts, or hopes."

CHAPTER 4

WHO YOU GONNA CALL

Hope beyond hope

'Ghostbusters', a movie released in 1984 became a cult classic with its catchphrase' 'Who you gonna call?'. When you are in a crisis, when things are beyond your control, who you gonna call?

Mark Twain is quoted as saying: 'There are only two certainties in life: death and taxes.' However, the inevitability of pain, suffering and crises are as certain as death and seem to occur with the frequency of taxes.

Life is full of challenges. Some little, some big, and for the most part we learn how to cope with these ups and downs, highs and lows. But every now and then we are confronted by genuine crisis. Things over which we have no control. Situations that overwhelm us. Circumstances which we seem hopelessly powerless to change. People lose jobs, houses, businesses. We face sickness, disease, poverty, abuse, mortality. Things that are unwanted, unwarranted, undeserved confront us and at the time it seems like there is no solution and no escaping from these realities.

The issue is these things not only cause us pain but they leave us vulnerable and exposed and the only options if something is beyond our ability to control or change is to either give up or to ask for help. But the question remains, who do you turn to? Who you gonna call?

Family? In many cases family is at the center of the issue. Friend? Our peers and associates often lack the experience and wisdom to offer real solutions. Most people lack the knowledge or the power to effect real change on our behalf. They are empathetic and compassionate, giving encouragement, trying to instill hope and belief that things will change with time and sometimes they do.

But in most cases our very darkest moments come when we are by ourselves. Alone with our thoughts, our problems. When the crisis seems to be at its deepest, overwhelming with no solution in sight, there is no one to talk to, no one to help. This becomes the moment of true decision. Times of crisis are times of profound change and the decisions we make in the worst moments of our lives have a huge effect in determining the person we become and the direction we take.

Some people might swear and curse at their misfortune. Some people might eventually turn to friends and family. Some may even seek professional help, if it is available. But for Jabez, there did not seem to be a natural answer to his predicament or his pain. Family and friends, if he had any, were the root cause of the problem and no help in finding a viable solution. Psychiatrists and counselors weren't invented yet. So Jabez did what multitudes have done throughout the course of human history. He turned to God and he prayed.

1 Chronicles 4:10

"And Jabez called to Elohim (the God) of Israel…"

Even before Jabez prayed. Before he made any request for deliverance or change. He had to make a decision as to who he was going to turn to.

Before you pray and beyond what you pray, you are going to make the most crucial decision of your life - Who are you gonna call? Who are you going to turn to? Who are you going to trust? This is the decision many people are confronted with in the most vulnerable moments of their life?

Jabez turned to Elohim - the God of Israel. Now Jabez could have turned to any god or appealed to any higher power, as many do. Within Israel and the surrounding cultures there was a plethora of deities to which appeal could have been made. '*El*' was the generic name for God, used among a number of ancient cultures, in fact it describes any god, any deity, but God did not reveal Himself as '*El*' to the Israelites, nor did Jabez turn to '*El*' and cry out to any god. He does not turn to wherever or whatever might bring him relief or comfort, but only to the Elohim of Israel. There is that to which you can turn that may bring temporary relief and even a measure of release, but ask yourself, is it temporary relief you are looking for or are you wanting real and lasting change?

So to whom did Jabez call? Who was the '*Elohim of Israel*'? To understand this we must first understand that within the Hebrew language there are no capital letters to distinguish, let's say, a higher power from a lesser one. We used 'God' or 'GOD' to distinguish the supreme being from a lesser deity, 'god'. The Hebrews did this by adding the plural ending 'im'.

Through the use of this plurality we have often been led to believe this is a reference to the triune nature of the Godhead - God the Father, God the Son and God the Holy Spirit - but this is not the case. Most of the time when this noun is used in the Hebrew for the true God it has singular masculine verbs. That is, 'He is' Elohim/God, not 'They are' Elohim/God. This is contrary to rules of Hebrew grammar and might I say English grammar as well.

When used of the true God, "Elohim" denotes what is called a plural of majesty, honor, or fullness. That is, He is GOD in the fullest sense of the word. Now we could say that each culture or each religion had or has their Elohim, their supreme or almighty god. But the claim here is that the Elohim of Israel was the God above all other gods. He is "GOD of gods" or literally, "ELOHIM of elohim" (Deut 10:17; Ps 136:2).

Psalms 86:8-10 New International Version (NIV)
Among the gods there is none like You, Lord; no deeds can compare with Yours. All the nations You have made will come and worship before You, Lord; they will bring glory to Your name. For You are great and do marvelous deeds; You alone are God.

This is the One that Jabez's heart cries out to. This is the One to whom he turns and commits his life and his future to - the Elohim of Israel. The only true God. The God above all gods. This is his trust. This is his hope. This was his conscious and deliberate choice. His calling on Elohim is more than a simple prayer, it is before anything else a declaration of his faith and a commitment of his life to fully trust God and to wholly follow Him.

Through the simple act of praying he is making a choice and a commitment to God, the Elohim of Israel.

Jabez turns to the One who is declared to be greater than all others, to the Name that is above every name. The power that is greater than all powers. He, from the beginning of His prayer, declares his faith and allegiance to only One.

Acts 4:12 Living Bible (TLB)
"There is salvation in no one else! Under all heaven there is no other name for men to call upon to save them."

In the moment of crisis, you are going to make a call, whether by default or by deliberate choice. Is your call to allow fate: 'Que sera, sera - whatever will be, will be', to determine your course, your future.

When you face your darkest moments, when you are confronted by your deepest fears, where are you going to turn? Who are you gonna call? Are you going to turn to whatever or whoever might offer a glimmer of hope or relief? Or are you like Jabez are you going to place your hope and trust in the One who is above all others?

Now I am not suggesting here that there are not other agencies that are needed or helpful in our times of crisis. I am not suggesting we don't need the support of family and friends at all times and especially in times of crisis. I am not saying we should not seek out professional help. These can be part of the process that God uses to heal and restore us. But I am saying that there are dimensions of life and change that can only come from God. No one and nothing can substitute for the peace of God that passes all understanding. (Philippians 4:7). There is no power in heaven or on earth equal to the power of God to bring transformation and restoration. Nothing can surpass the love of God, the mercy of God, the forgiveness of God. Nothing brings hope like the promises of God. There is no substitute for that sense of purpose that comes from a relationship with God. God alone can make all things work together for your good to achieve His purposes in your life and to enable you to live to your fullest potential.

Without faith and trust we limit the answer to life's greatest challenges to human ingenuity and resources and as great as these are, they are limited, and in many cases of crisis powerless to bring real hope and effect real change. But there is One who gives hope to the hopeless and grace to those who need and seek His help. (Hebrews 4:16) Only One can make possible what is otherwise impossible.

As it was for Jabez, so it is for us, it is a choice: Who are you going to call? Who are you going to trust in the most vulnerable moments of your life? Is the darkness of those times going to overwhelm you and consume you to the point where life is without hope and without meaning? Or is there real power in prayer? I have been there, in those dark times. I have also known many, many others, who have been there. I have personally seen the tragedy and the trauma that comes when people lose all hope and give up on life. But thankfully, I have also witnessed the marvelous and the miraculous transformation that is possible and has happened when people have turned to God and prayed.

Who is going to be the source of your hope and trust? Who has the power to work within you infinitely beyond anything you can ask or pray for?

Trusting God and experiencing the transformative and restorative power of God through prayer is as real and uplifting as the crises of life are deep and depressing. Jabez didn't abandon God and blame God in his time of crisis he turned to God and he prayed. God heard his cry, answered his prayer and transformed his life.

That is the invitation I extend to you right now. That is the invitation of heaven and the promise.

James 4:8 Living Bible (TLB)
When you draw close to God, God will draw close to you.

Psalm 34:18-19 Living Bible (TLB)
18 The Lord is close to those whose hearts are breaking; He rescues those who are humbly sorry for their sins. 19 The good man does not escape all troubles—he has them too. But the Lord helps him in each and every one.

Psalm 145:18-19 New International Version (NIV)
18 The Lord is near to all who call on Him,
to all who call on Him in truth.
19 He fulfills the desires of those who fear Him;
He hears their cry and saves them.

Romans 10:13 New International Version (NIV)
"Everyone who calls on the name of the Lord will be saved."

Acts 4:12 Living Bible (TLB)
"There is salvation in no one else! Under all heaven there is
no other name for men to call upon to save them."

Romans 10:9-10 New International Version (NIV)
9 If you declare with your mouth, "Jesus is Lord," and believe in
your heart that God raised him from the dead, you will be saved.
10 For it is with your heart that you believe and are justified, and
it is with your mouth that you profess your faith and are saved.

There is hope beyond your hopelessness and help beyond your helplessness. Genuine prayer brings real answers.

Who you gonna call? Call today! Call now!

For this is God's promise and commitment to you:

Ephesians 3:20 Living Bible (TLB)
20 Now glory be to God, who by His mighty power at work within us
is able to do far more than we would ever dare to ask or even dream
of—infinitely beyond our highest prayers, desires, thoughts, or hopes.

CHAPTER 5
NO LIMITS

Hope is a light in dark places.

Hope is a powerful motivation. It can be defined as a positive expectation for the future. There is little that is more exciting and uplifting than the realization that what we have hoped for, prayed for or dreamed of has become a reality. Equally there is nothing that we find more disappointing and depressing than when our expectations fail to materialize.

Jabez prayer is the expression of his hopes and dreams for his future, the promise and the possibility of what could be. This hope fills us, as it did with him, with an excitement and anticipation as it dares us to believe that better and more and change are possible. But the reality of life experience also gives us a sense of fear and trepidation because it teaches us that not everything, in fact hardly anything, ever goes exactly as we hoped or planned. So we are confronted with one of life's constant dilemmas: Do we allow the dictates of our life experience to keep us from the possibility of what could be or do we accept the challenge to pursue the dream of a life 'Beyond Ordinary'? Knowing full well, we will face challenges and encounter opposition and obstacles which will seek not only to hinder us but to obliterate the dream all together and make us feel as if this life was meant for others but not for me.

The choices Jabez faced and the decisions he had to make were not make believe, they were real life dilemmas and decisions and His prayer contains some real wisdom in how we can face these same challenges and manage the expectations we have that will have a considerable bearing on the outcome of our pursuit.

The expectations we have around any of our hopes or dreams are centered on two aspects of our beliefs: 1) what we believe God or fate will bring our way, and, 2) what we believe we can and will contribute to our endeavors.

The expectation we impose on our dream will
largely determine whether it lives or dies.

Jabez prayer is particularly insightful into these aspects of life. So as we begin the journey of looking at the actual prayer of Jabez I want us to take a moment and look at the prayer as a whole and see what it can teach us before we look at each aspect of the prayer in detail.

1 Chronicles 4:10
(transliterated from the Hebrew of the Masoretic Text)
"And Jabez called to Elohim (the God) of Israel saying, 'If only with blessing will You continue to bless me and will You greatly increase my territory and may it come to pass by Your hand with me that You will make me out from this evil without shaping me with the way of pain.' And to bring it into being Elohim (God) granted that which he asked for."

What is so special about this prayer that it attracted the attention of God and caused Him to respond to it and grant Jabez what he requested and then turn around and have it recorded so we could learn from it as well? What is so unusual about this prayer that preachers have been talking about it for centuries?

The prayer itself seems to be patterned off of God's Promise to Abraham and his descendants, of which Jabez was one.

Genesis 12:1-3 New International Version (NIV)
*"The Lord had said to Abram, "Go from your country, your people
and your father's household to the land I will show you.*
'I will make you into a great nation,
and I will bless you;
I will make your name great,
and you will be a blessing.
I will bless those who bless you,
and whoever curses you I will curse;
and all peoples on earth
will be blessed through you.' "

God's covenant promise to Abraham was that if he would leave his past behind and follow and trust God then God would bless him, give him a land that he and his descendants would possess and that He would make him all that he could become and greater than he believed was possible.

It seems to me that Jabez began to understand that this promise wasn't just something given to Abrham hundreds of years earlier but it was for him and his generation and he began to take it and apply it personally to his own life and circumstance.

And so it is with the Word of God and the promises of God, they are for each of us personally and they apply to each of us and our circumstances. The promises and purposes of God are not ancient history or myth or legend, they are relevant and applicable to you and your life and they possess the same power of change for you as they did for Jabez when God answered his prayer.

But as we just mentioned the prayer as a whole gives us powerful insight into managing our hopes and dreams and how and what we expect to happen throughout the unfolding of the promise. I want you to see something remarkable about this prayer and the man who prayed it.

There are two notable attributes of this prayer as we look at it as a whole.

It is a Prayer without Qualifications

To me the first notable aspect of Jabez prayer is that of Jabez expectation of God. The first thing I want you to notice is that Jabez is not specific in the sense that he does not qualify or quantify any of his requests. By that, I mean he did not specify how he wanted God to bless him. He doesn't ask for a wife or a new home, a better job with more money. He doesn't ask for more oxen or a new chariot. He doesn't say what territory he wants God to give him. There are no specifics about what he expects the hand of God to do in his life, and there is no list of evil that he wants God to keep him from.

It seems that he went to God with no preconceived ideas about how and what and when God was going to work in his life. He prayed with an open heart, an open mind and an open hand. He was open to any and all of the Divine possibilities.

I think one of our greatest mistakes is that we often go to God with our lists of what we want and when we want it. Our prayers more often resemble a protest march (What do we want? .... When do we want it? NOW!) then they do a whole hearted seeking after God. Often our prayer is bringing God down to our level of expectation, to the limits of our thinking and what we believe is possible. We expect God to meet us on our terms and to fulfill our expectations of Him. Instead of praying in a way that exposes our lives to what God thinks and what He makes possible.

Isaiah 55:8-11 New International Version (NIV)
8 "For My thoughts are not your thoughts,
neither are your ways My ways,"
declares the Lord.
9 "As the heavens are higher than the earth,
so are My ways higher than your ways
and My thoughts than your thoughts.
10 As the rain and the snow
come down from heaven,
and do not return to it
without watering the earth
and making it bud and flourish,
so that it yields seed for the sower and bread for the eater,
11 so is My word that goes out from My mouth:
It will not return to Me empty,
but will accomplish what I desire
and achieve the purpose for which I sent it."

This again poses two possibilities:

The first is that Jabez does not know all that he needs or how to even pray effectively for what he needs.

All he knows is that to be the person he wants to be, each of these aspects of God's grace seems to be necessary. He realizes that he has no idea what these blessings will look like or how or when they will come.

Romans 8:26-28 Living Bible (TLB)

"And in the same way—by our faith—the Holy Spirit helps us with our daily problems and in our praying. For we don't even know what we should pray for nor how to pray as we should, but the Holy Spirit prays for us with such feeling that it cannot be expressed in words. 27 And the Father who knows all hearts knows, of course, what the Spirit is saying as he pleads for us in harmony with God's own will. 28 And we know that all that happens to us is working for our good if we love God and are fitting into his plans."

The second possibility is that Jabez does not want to limit God and the possibilities of what God can do to the level of his imagination or expectations.

I would like to think he was smart enough to realize both truths.

To be the type of people we desire to be, the first thing we have to realize is that none of us has the knowledge, foresight or wisdom to ask for all that we truly need. Secondly, none of us truly knows God well enough to know all that He can or will do for us.

How many of us have become conditioned to thinking that God will only do what we can believe for and ask for in prayer. If God's grace and power were limited to the level of our actual faith, do you know how small our worlds would be? When God said, *"If you have faith as a grain of mustard seed",* (Matthew 17:20), I think He deliberately chose one of the smallest visible things He could, so we would realize that He is not relying on anything we can do or pray for or believe for, but even with the slightest glimpse of faith, He can unleash His goodness and grace in our lives and we can see the impossible happen.

To limit our lives to our level of expectation, that is, what we think is possible is to put us in danger of becoming short-sighted and small minded. But, if we want to be those who rise to the heights that God can lift us we cannot afford to limit God to our level of thinking, desires or even prayers. We have to become a people who know God well enough to know *"(He truly) is able to do far more than we would ever dare to ask or even dream of— infinitely beyond our highest prayers, desires, thoughts, or hopes."* (Ephesians 3:20 Living Bible (TLB))

In his prayer, Jabez refuses to limit his life to what he could imagine or dream of or even believe was possible. Rather, his prayer displays an openness that exposes his life, his future, his destiny totally to God.

When we believe that our future and our destiny is reliant on the specifics of our prayers and limited to the level of our faith, life becomes hard work and we often develop a mentality that we have to almost beg God for anything and everything we want or need.

On the other hand when we know how great, how good and how gracious God is and that He is the One endlessly working to bring us into the fullness of His plans and purposes. Then we move from a life ruled by religious thought and demeanor to one of a relationship with God in which we simply walk with Him, trusting and believing that He not only knows what is best for us, but He is actually working to bring it pass.

Secondly: It is a Prayer without Conditions

The prayer is birthed with the words that mark a vow, *'If only'*. But a vow is typically reciprocal, **IF** you will do this and this **THEN** I will do this. (cf. Genesis 28:20-22; Judges 11:30-31)

Genesis 28:20-22 New International Version (NIV)
*"Then Jacob made a vow, saying, 'If God will … **then** … I will … .'"*

If you read the context of this story God promises to Jacob are unconditional. Yet Jacob in his response places conditions on himself that God didn't ask for. God simply states that He will act for Jacob's good and He asks Jacob for nothing in return.

Why is it that when God promises that He is going to do good things in our life and bless us and keep us that we then feel that we need to put conditions or expectations on ourselves that show God how grateful we are or how good we are going to be in response to His blessing?

Why do we feel we need to somehow manipulate God into doing what He has already promised us He will? I wonder, is it because we all grow up in an environment where manipulation is such commonplace. 'If you clean your room up, then we will …'. 'If you don't let me go out tonight, I am never going to speak to you again.' We want things, others want things and so we enter into this whole realm of bartering and bargaining and manipulation and we end up transferring this level of thinking, this level of emotional insecurity into our relationship with God.

But, Jabez didn't do that. This prayer begins with the 'IF ONLY' but it is totally devoid of the "THEN'. Maybe Jabez realized he was a screw up and that whatever he promised God he would do, he more than likely wouldn't. Maybe he realized he had failed in the past and that he would fail again in the future. Maybe he just dared to believe that God was that much bigger and better than he was. Whatever the case Jabez didn't feel the need to try and manipulate God into doing what he was asking for and neither do you. Much of the time God gives us what we need unconditionally, because it has been bought and paid for by the blood of the cross. Whenever there are conditions, it's not that God is trying to limit us and keep His blessing from us. It is to position us in such a way that when we receive what He has for us we will be able to keep it, enjoy it and walk in it.

Our success is not reliant on what we can do for God
but solely on what He does for us and in us.

Some of you are limiting God because you have tried to tell God how and when and with what He should bless you. You have told God what He needs to do in order for you to be happy and successful and when it has not happened the way you expected you somehow felt that God didn't listen to you or that God doesn't love you as much as He loves someone else.

Some of you are limiting God by trying to live up to a set of self-imposed expectations. Because God has blessed you in the past or maybe just because He saved you, you have told God how you were going to live and what you were going to do to show Him how grateful you were. You failed and therefore you believe that you don't deserve more of what God has for you or that He doesn't want to give you more.

The problem we have is that we cannot believe that anyone, not even God can be so good, can be so gracious and love us so deeply that they would pursue our best interest without imposing on us limits and conditions and that He would somehow cause us to to settle for less than what we should and to become less than the person we could have been.

The prayer of Jabez and my prayer for you today is:

DON'T LIMIT GOD TO WHAT YOU CAN THINK OF, DREAM OF OR BELIEVE FOR. KNOW THAT HE IS BIGGER AND BETTER THAN YOU WILL EVER FULLY UNDERSTAND. HIS POWER IS GREATER. HIS LOVE STRONGER. HIS GRACE MORE THAN SUFFICIENT FOR ANY AND ALL YOU WILL EVER NEED FOR YOU TO REALIZE YOUR POTENTIAL AND TO FULFILL THE PLAN AND THE PURPOSE GOD HAS FOR YOU. LEARN TO LIVE AND PRAY AS JABEZ DID, OPEN ENDED. OPEN TO ALL GOD HAS FOR YOU WITHOUT QUALIFICATION. WITHOUT CONDITIONS. NO LIMITS.

Ephesians 3:15-20 Living Bible (TLB)

"When I think of the wisdom and scope of His plan, I fall down on my knees and pray to the Father … 16 that out of His glorious, unlimited resources He will give you the mighty inner strengthening of his Holy Spirit. 17 And I pray that Christ will be more and more at home in your hearts, living within you as you trust in Him. May your roots go down deep into the soil of God's marvelous love; 18-19 and may you be able to feel and understand, as all God's children should, how long, how wide, how deep, and how high His love really is; and to experience this love for yourselves, though it is so great that you will never see the end of it or fully know or understand it. And so at last you will be filled up with God Himself. 20 Now glory be to God, who by His mighty power at work within us is able to do far more than we would ever dare to ask or even dream of—infinitely beyond our highest prayers, desires, thoughts, or hopes."

CHAPTER 6

THE 'X' FACTOR

Have you ever sat down and thought about what it would take to make you happy? Have you dreamt of the things that would give you a sense of fulfillment? Have you ever said, 'If only I had that', or 'If only this would happen'? Well that is exactly how Jabez begins his prayer. If only! We all dream of a better life. We all desire things that we believe would make our lives better. There are things - possessions, circumstances - you would like to have, that you desire to have, because IF ONLY you had those things they would radically change your life.

The intense desire for a better life drives most people. We deeply desire things to be better than they are, even if they are good, and certainly, more often than not, better than they have been in our past. We dream of and desire things that will improve or change the way we do life. We long for and search for those things that we think will give purpose, meaning and significance to our life. We often look for these in material things like possessions and money which can give us a sense of security and achievement. So much so that the idea behind this first aspect of Jabez prayer: *'If only with blessing will You continue to bless me ...'* (1 Chronicles 4:10), has been reduced to the acquisition of material possessions. Now I am not saying that blessing does not include material benefits, but I do think that if we only see it in that light we are going to miss much of what we are meant to derive from Jabez prayer. This prayer of Jabez is about far more than 'blessing' and 'property' or should I say that his request for blessing and territory goes far deeper than just material possessions.

It is easy for most of us to identify with this aspect of the prayer because like Jabez, we want the same thing for the same reasons. Our lack, our limitations, our shortcomings, our weaknesses, our pain and suffering bring us to the realization that in order to experience the reality of the life that we so deeply desire there are dimensions of life that we desperately need and must seek after.

So the question arises: When Jabez uttered this prayer what was he really asking God for?

Was he simply asking God to ease the burden of his past and his pain? Was he asking God for something that would enhance his lifestyle and make his life better or more secure?

The request for blessing has become, in modern thought, associated with the 'prosperity gospel' where God is reduced to the agent of fulfilling our desires, our wants, our needs, but this is a far cry from what the Biblical term 'blessing' really means.

What Jabez was asking for and what we understand and are asking for when we pray these same words, I believe, are vastly different.

The prayer of Jabez, in many english translations, begins with these words:

'Oh, that You would bless me indeed'.

Now in the original Hebrew language there is no expression of intensity, like 'indeed', or 'greatly' and the translation from Hebrew into English does nothing to capture the heart of Jabez nor the intensity of his prayer.

This phrase in Hebrew is: *"im bāra<u>k</u> bāra<u>k</u>"* and could be literal translated: *if blessing, blessing. 'Im'* speaks of a desire, a longing, a want, a need.

We might use a term like 'if only' to describe a level of seeking or longing. If only this would happen. If only I could have this. It is a wishing, a wanting for something to change.

The double call of blessing, blessing brings a tone of desperation and an expression of intensity to the desire. There is within the beginning of Jabez's prayer a desperation that resonates like the deep and desperate cry of one searching for that which is missing and lost. It is not like, 'Oh, I have lost my keys. If only I could find my keys.' Or 'I'm hungry, if only I had a hamburger.' It is more likened to the anguished and harrowing cry of a mother whose child has been missing for days or even longer and cannot be found and she on bended knees cries from the depth of her being their name over and over again, desperately longing, seeking and hoping for their return.

The depth of this cry of Jabez's heart might best be understood when compared with another prayer in Scripture that imitates the intensity and desperation of this double expression. The harrowing cry comes from Jesus himself as He utters his dying words from the cross:

Matthew 27:46 New International Version (NIV)
"Jesus cried out in a loud voice, 'Eli, Eli, lema sabachthani?' (which means 'My God, my God, why have you forsaken me?')."

Both are cries of utter desperation that come from within one who has a deep sense that they have been forsaken or abandoned by God Himself. Yet the extraordinary thing about Jabez and Jesus, unlike so many who feel abandoned by God and grow bitter and blame God for their circumstance, they both, in the midst of their darkest moment and deepest anguish, turn to God as the answer to their need. They cry out in utter desperation for only that which He can supply. Jabez, like his Saviour many years later, doesn't abandon his faith in God because of the circumstances of his life but makes this deliberate decision to turn to God and to plead with God as the only One who can truly supply that which he lacks, that which he longs for.

To treat this prayer in any way as a formula for success or prosperity, we might suggest that it be accompanied by the same intensity of desire and driven by the same deep sense of lostness and longing as found in Jabez. Perhaps the reason so many are confined to ordinary is that we never reach that level of desire and desperation where we cry out with the longing and intensity that brings a response from heaven.

For Jabez there was a dimension of life that was encapsulated within the promises of God, but had never materialized in the reality of his experience. We have all experienced this to some degree. We have the promise, we see the possibility of what could be, we have the dream of the way things were meant to be, but life seems to have cast a dark shadow over this reality so that it remains only an illusion. Something that seems to be there, but always lurking just out of sight or just out of reach. Something that you never quite seem to be able to grasp. The dream that never becomes a reality.

So the prayer of Jabez begins with this cry to God, for a dimension of life that was lost or missing and that Jabez was desperately seeking for. A dimension of life that would fundamentally change who he was and the life he seemed compelled to endure because of the circumstance of his birth and upbringing.

But again we ask the question: 'What was Jabez asking for when he cries out, *"If only with blessing will You continue to bless me... ."*?'

In the first instance we need to understand that in the Hebrew language the word *'barak'* means to kneel, to bless. When we bless God we kneel, we humble ourselves before Him. When we ask for or seek the blessing of God it has the connotation of positioning ourselves before God by kneeling in honor and surrender to Him. We see this in many traditions where one is favored, honored or blessed by another; the one receiving the blessing kneels before the one conferring the blessing.

Hebrews 7:7 New International Version (NIV)
'And without doubt the lesser is blessed by the greater.'

To ask for blessing and to be blessed is to first recognise that there is one greater than you that has the power and the means to convey the blessing you seek..

And to kneel, to bend the knee has deeper connotations than what many of us realize. The knee is one of the weakest parts of the body. The expression for being fearful is to be "weak at the knees." We know that one of the most common and debilitating sports injuries are knee injuries. It is in the recognition of our limitations, our lack, our weaknesses that we bend our knee. It is in this place of vulnerability, as we are brought low by our circumstances and the dictates of life, that we have the unique opportunity to kneel before God and it is through the power of His blessing that we receive the wisdom, the strength and the power that allows us to rise and to enter new levels of our potential and purpose. It is the blessing of God that enables us to overcome our own inherent weaknesses and failures and to achieve what would not otherwise be possible. Thus God's blessing is His empowerment to be able to do what is not within our natural capabilities to do or that which is limited by our personal circumstance.

If we return to Genesis 1 where God first declares blessing over His creation, we read:

Genesis 1:20-28 New Living Translation (NLT)
"20 Then God said, 'Let the waters swarm with fish and other life. Let the skies be filled with birds of every kind.' ... 22 **Then God blessed them, saying, 'Be fruitful and multiply.'** *... 24 .... And that is what happened. ... 26 Then God said, 'Let Us make human beings in our image, to be like Us.' ... 27 So God created human beings in His own image. In the image of God He created them; male and female He created them. 28* **Then God blessed them and said, 'Be fruitful and multiply.'** *"*

Here we find that when God declared blessing over His creation, whether mankind or animal, His decree was His empowerment to fulfill their created purpose and develop and mature to fulfill their God given potential.

God, by His will and power creates an environment in which each species can develop their potential and fulfill their purpose. He placed fish in the sea, birds in the air, man and various animals on land. Each by His favor and power is granted the ability to achieve what they were created for.

While after the fall we encounter all kinds of opposition and obstacles to our development, to the achievement of our true purpose and potential, it is still the blessing of God that makes possible that which seems impossible.

While we might see God's blessing as any level of good fortune, life teaches us that it is possible to become rich, famous or powerful without living in a relationship with God that brings His blessing. The testimony of many also tells us that you can achieve any or all of these and still have a life devoid of purpose and meaning. You cannot, in all truth, become the person you were meant to be or do those things that you are created and called to do apart from the blessing of God. So this is what Jabez cried out for. This is what He longed for. This is that which is missing in His life.

That favor and power to live a life filled with divine purpose and to achieve the fullness of his potential.

For Jabez the request for blessing was more than a request for the good fortune or favor that might come to pass through natural providence. In the Hebrew understanding and in Jabez 'mind, blessing was the outflow of a life lived in right relationship with God. You either lived in covenant relationship with God where you were committed to keeping His Law and observing His ways (Deuteronomy 28) and were blessed or you did not obey God His Word or follow His ways and the result was the way of the curse.

His cry and his bowing of the knee was alone to the One who could supply his need. True blessing only has one source. There is only one God who has the power and the grace to release in you and to give you all that you need to become the person you were created to be.

So Jabez cries to the true and almighty God for all and only that which He can bring into being.

2 Peter 1:3-4, The Passion Translation (TPT)

"Everything we could ever need for life and complete devotion to God has already been deposited in us by His divine power. For all this was lavished upon us through the rich experience of knowing Him who has called us by name and invited us to come to Him through a glorious manifestation of His goodness. 4 As a result of this, He has given you magnificent promises that are beyond all price, so that through the power of these tremendous promises you can experience partnership with the divine nature, by which you have escaped the corrupt desires that are of the world."

It is through our relationship with God in Jesus Christ we become partakers of everything that He promises us including protection, provision, wisdom, knowledge and whatever other measures of His grace and power that we need to become the person we are called to be and live a life of purposes, continually growing and maturing to realize more and more of the potential He has invested in us.

So blessing is not only that which comes from the cry of a desperate heart but that which comes from a bowing of the knee and committing to live one's life in a covenant relationship with God and in doing so discovering that dimension of His fullness that we are lacking in the natural and so desperately longing for in order to be enabled to fulfill the purpose and potential of our life.

When Jabez prayed for blessing, he was not asking for a sudden miraculous change, he was asking God to journey with Him and he was committing to journey with God, where the course and destiny of his life would be determined by the plans, purposes and promises of God rather than by the fears, frustrations and fate or fortunes that the circumstance that life would dictate.

You see the journey of life is a journey of choice, not once not twice, but every day making the decision of who or what is going to dictate or determine the direction and destiny of your life.

While there are many specific moments of blessing, blessing was never intended to be an event. God intended it to be a way of living. So this first aspect of Jabez prayer is that God would take him beyond the limitations or capabilities of his natural self and circumstance. To take him beyond the dictates of a life lived within the uncertainty and insecurity of the realm of fate and to enable him to live a life that was intentionally and deliberately lived within the guidelines of God's will and God's Word. Jabez prayer was asking that God's covenant promises would ultimately be that which determined the course and the outcome of his life.

We can seek for the so-called blessed life in that which people and circumstances can bring. We can hope or pray for that degree of favor or fortune which might ease some of our burdens or enhance some aspect of our lifestyle. But from Jabez' experience, neither the people he knew nor the circumstances he had experienced had to this point delivered that hope. He had, as is the reality of many, experienced disappointment, hurt, frustration and pain, almost to the point of being devoid of all hope, where the prospect of life was not that of favor or fortune but only that of continued tyranny, of more suffering and more pain.

So when Jabez prayed for blessing he was asking for much, much more than that which would lift his burden or enhance his lifestyle. From the outset the prayer was the desperate cry of Jabez 'heart for that life which only heaven could supply.

This is where the prayer of Jabez begins, with a deep cry of his heart for change. But he also knew that change involved more than a prayer request, not just with a **cry** from his heart but a **commitment** of his life to live in relationship with the only One who had the true power of transformation.

This prayer is not a formula for success, it is a cry for change. It may come from a deep sense of being abandoned by God, but in the end it is a prayer, a bending of the knee in surrender to the only One who has the power of change and it is an unreserved commitment to live in surrender and obedience to God. To live, not just by the promises of God, but by all the principles and precepts that would enable Jabez and us to live our best life.

Ephesians 3:20 Living Bible (TLB)

"Now glory be to God, who by His mighty power at work within us is able to do far more than we would ever dare to ask or even dream of—infinitely beyond our highest prayers, desires, thoughts, or hopes."

CHAPTER 7

'MORE' 'MORE' - NOTHING LESS

The great danger of the human life is not that we seek
for too much but that we settle for too little.

1 Chronicles 4:10

(transliterated from the Hebrew of the Masoretic Text)
And Jabez called to Elohim (the God) of Israel saying, '...
will You greatly increase my territory ...And to bring it into
being Elohim (God) <u>granted</u> that which he asked for."

'More - More'. The quest for more has become the all consuming pursuit of so many in today's world. More to make us happier. More so I can be successful. More so I can be fulfilled. Jabez is asking for more land, more possessions and God gives it to him. Here we have that conundrum as to when is enough, enough. When does prosperity become greed? Where do we draw the line between sufficiency and selfishness, between consumerism and contentment? As we read this aspect of Jabez prayer we can quickly be drawn into the arguments that revolve around the issue of prosperity and enter into that internal tug-of-war between self indulgence and self denial. Some use these types of verses as justification for a level of self indulgence, a seeking for increase, 'more blessing', 'more possessions', 'more stuff'. Others immediately recoil and pull back for fear of being seen as self centered and greedy. Both of these views, while having some measure of validity, miss the mark entirely in what Jabez was asking God for.

When Jabez asked God for more territory, it was not primarily about possessions nor property or even prosperity, it was about God's promises. God had promised Israel the land as an inheritance and each family a portion in it, but the previous generations had settled for less than the fullness of what God had promised.

Joshua 13:1-2, New King James Version (NKJV)
"Now Joshua was old, advanced in years. And the Lord said to him: 'You are old, advanced in years, and there remains very much land yet to be possessed.' "

The result of this was that Jabez and his generation still had to fight to enter into the fullness of the promises and provision of God that were lacking because of the failure of the previous generations to appropriate all that God had promised them. When the challenges became too great, they grew weary. They stopped fighting to lay hold of what God had promised. They came to a place where they accepted and settled for what they already had. While we can be critical of them isn't this the same challenge we face. Isn't it easier to settle for what we have rather than to push in and fight, not just for more of what God has promised but for 'ALL' that He has promised.

The problem for Israel and for us is when our preference for a lifestyle takes priority over our pursuit of the promise. When personal comfort or 'happiness' takes precedence over the challenges we must embrace and the hardships we must endure to fully enter into who we are called to be and what we are called to do. In fully embracing the plans and purposes of God the greater danger lies not in our desire for more but in our willingness to settle for less.

If comfort becomes our goal, or conformity to the thinking and opinions of those around us who tell us to settle down, to stop trying so hard, that we have done enough, that it can't be done or that we will never make it. If those become the voices that dictate our choices and determine our destiny then we will never become who we are called to be and we will never embrace the fullness of what God has promised us.

For many, prosperity has become an issue, in the negative sense. Because people have abused this truth to some degree in the past, we seek to avoid it. But to prosper simply means 'to push forward', 'to advance'. Surely this has to be the heart and the spirit of every fully devoted follower of Jesus Christ. To push forward, to advance and to embrace those levels of blessing that God has promised and provided for us. We must ask ourselves: 'Can I ever truly be content with less than the fullness of what God promises in His Word? Should we ever settle or be content with less than the fullness of the blessing Jesus brought on the cross with His own precious blood?'

2 Peter 1:3-4, The Passion Translation (TPT)

"Everything we could ever need for life and complete devotion to God has already been deposited in us by His divine power. For all this was lavished upon us through the rich experience of knowing Him who has called us by name and invited us to come to Him through a glorious manifestation of His goodness. 4 As a result of this, He has given you magnificent promises that are beyond all price, so that through the power of these tremendous promises you can experience partnership with the divine nature, by which you have escaped the corrupt desires that are of the world."

The challenge of Jabez and the challenge for us is that what we seek and what we pursue should never be dictated by this world and its priorities, by our own human nature and its desires, nor even by the perceptions or opinions of others. The reality is we have these tremendous promises of God that grant us the power to enter into and experience the fullness of His provision which in turn enables us to fulfill His purposes. These magnificent promises should be compelling us to new heights of not just more, but ALL. ALL that God has promised. ALL that I can be through the power that dwells in me. It is through His promises and His power that we have everything we need to live a life in complete devotion to Him.

To live a life beyond the ordinary the question is not just what are you willing to seek after but what are you willing to settle for?

We worry about the person who becomes consumed by greed when in reality I have seen far, far more people living in need and deprivation, in frustration and failure with regard to possessing the fullness of what God has promised and provided rather than those who possess it but use it for the wrong purpose.

Someone once said, *'Greed is never a problem of possession; it is a problem of purpose'.* When your dream is centered in fulfilling the purposes of God, when your dream is as big as God's plans you will always need more of God, more of God's blessing, more resources to do what you are called to do. The only limit I know is the limitation of the human spirit to fully pursue God and His plans and purposes for our life.

Again, we come back to that verse that says:

Ephesians 3:20 Living Bible (TLB)
*"God, who by His mighty power at work within us is able to do far
more than we would ever dare to ask or even dream of—infinitely
beyond our highest prayers, desires, thoughts, or hopes."*

There has never been a person born who can out dream God and what
He can do through the life of one who is fully devoted to Him.

We decide when we have had enough. We decide when we have reached
our limit. We decide when we have gone as far as we can go, but there is
more, in God there is always more.

"Enlarge my territory" is not just a prayer about possessions, it is a
prayer from a spirit and a heart that is seeking to enter into and to possess
the fullness of God. What made Jabez a stand out was that long before he
possessed anything of the fullness of God's promise for himself, while he
was still in his pain and deprevation, he possessed a different spirit. He had
a spirit and a heart that could not settle and would not settle for anything
less than the fullness of what God had promised. He didn't just want more,
he wanted ALL.

Perhaps, he was inspired by the story of one who had gone before him,
one of the heroes of faith, Caleb the son of Jephunneh. He was one of the
twelve who originally spied out the land under Moses' direction. Listen to
his story:

This is God's word over Caleb and His promise to Him after He
returned from spying out the land of Canaan.

Numbers 14:24, New King James Version (NKJV)
*"My servant Caleb, because he has a different spirit in him
and has followed Me fully, I will bring into the land where
he went, and his descendants shall inherit it."*

This is his story after 45 years of waiting for the timing of the fulfillment of that promise.

Joshua 14:6-15, New King James Version (NKJV)
*"6 Then the children of Judah came to Joshua in Gilgal. And Caleb the son
of Jephunneh the Kenizzite said to him: "You know the word which the Lord
said to Moses the man of God concerning you and me in Kadesh Barnea. 7 I
was forty years old when Moses the servant of the Lord sent me from Kadesh
Barnea to spy out the land, and I brought back word to him as it was in my
heart. 8 Nevertheless my brethren who went up with me made the heart of
the people melt, but I wholly followed the Lord my God. 9 So Moses swore on
that day, saying, 'Surely the land where your foot has trodden shall be your
inheritance and your children's forever, because you have wholly followed
the Lord my God.' 10 And now, behold, the Lord has kept me alive, as He
said, these forty-five years, ever since the Lord spoke this word to Moses while
Israel wandered in the wilderness; and now, here I am this day, eighty-five
years old. 11 As yet I am as strong this day as on the day that Moses sent me;
just as my strength was then, so now is my strength for war, both for going
out and for coming in. 12 Now therefore, give me this mountain of which
the Lord spoke in that day; for you heard in that day how the Anakim were
there, and that the cities were great and fortified. It may be that the Lord
will be with me, and I shall be able to drive them out as the Lord said."
13 And Joshua blessed him, and gave Hebron to Caleb the son of
Jephunneh as an inheritance. 14 Hebron therefore became the inheritance*

of Caleb the son of Jephunneh the Kenizzite to this day, because he wholly followed the Lord God of Israel. 15 And the name of Hebron formerly was Kirjath Arba (Arba was the greatest man among the Anakim)."

Few people are truly possessed by this different spirit. A spirit that wholly follows the Lord and one that refuses to settle for anything less than the fullness of what God has promised, but Jabez, like Caleb before him, was one of them.

He was not graced with some special ability. He was not favored in his upbringing or the circumstance of his life, he was simply possessed of a different spirit. He could not be content with some or even for much of the good things that God had promised and had already provided - he didn't just want more, he wanted all.

This spirit not only allows us to enter into a life beyond our lack, beyond our limitations, but to enter a life that allows us to realize our potential and become all we can be. This spirit brings release to those around us and it builds a platform from which the next generation can launch without fighting for that which was meant to be their inheritance. As we have said, one of the reasons Jabez prayed this prayer was because the previous generation had not claimed the fullness of what God has promised them and so Jabez prays that he might become the possessor of those promises.

If there is more of the kingdom to be embraced can we afford to pray for anything less than what Jabez prayed. Can we afford to pray for anything less than the development of our full potential? Can we afford to pray with anything other than that spirit which fully, wholly embraces the purpose and promises of God. If my heart and desire is to glorify God and advance His Kingdom should I not seek to build the best platform I possibly can for the next generation.

The challenge we all face and the question we must all ask is: Am I pursuing the fullness of God, His promises and His purposes for my life or am I growing weary and allowing the circumstances of my life to begin to dictate my future and my destiny?

Are the challenges I am facing causing me to settle and accept life as it is or are the promises and declarations of God inspiring me to stand up, to push forward and advance to become all and do all that God has created and called me for?

Enlarge my territory, is not a plea for more, it is a heart cry for ALL, all God has promised and provided. It's a spirit that refuses to settle, that cannot be content with less than the fullness of God.

2 Peter 1:4,3, The Passion Translation (TPT)
"He has given you magnificent promises that are beyond all price, so that through the power of these tremendous promises you can experience …
everything (you) could ever need for life and complete devotion to God."
Who you become and what you do will ultimately be
determined by what you seek after or what you settle for.

The dictates of circumstance will demand you settle for less. The promise will declare there is more and demand that you seek for more.

Don't settle for less. Don't be content with some or even much. Jabez prayer is God, enlarge my territory so I can embrace the fullness of your promises and the fulness of your purpose for my life. Nothing less!

Ephesians 3:20 Living Bible (TLB)
*"Now glory be to God, who by His mighty power at work within us **is**
able to do far more than we would ever dare to ask or even dream*
of—infinitely beyond our highest prayers, desires, thoughts, or hopes."

CHAPTER 8

THE TURNING

1 Chronicles 4:9-10
(transliterated from the Hebrew of the Masoretic Text)
*"Now it came to pass, Jabez was honored more than his brethren and his
mother called his name Jabez saying, 'because I brought forth in pain'.
And Jabez called to Elohim (the God) of Israel saying, '... may it
come to pass by Your hand with me that You will make me out
from this evil without shaping me with the way of pain.' "*

The traditional translation of the third part of Jabez prayer reads:

1 Chronicles 4:10 New American Standard Bible
*"... that Your hand might be with me, and that You
would keep me from harm so that it would not hurt me!"*

Or alternately:

1 Chronicles 4:10 New King James Version
*"... that Your hand would be with me, and that You would
keep me from evil, that I may not cause pain!"*

The latter is a very noble thought, 'keep me from evil, so I won't hurt others'. The old adage, 'hurt people hurt people.' So Jabez prays that he won't be hurt or harmed anymore by evil and that this way of pain won't continue to shape him and that he won't shape other's through his pain and then it says that God answered Jabez prayer.

"God granted him that which he asked for."

If we honestly believed that we could pray this type of prayer and that God would answer it, I am convinced that there would be multitudes of people on bended knees, praying these words right now. I mean, if there was even a chance that I could escape from the evil and pain of my past, if there was the remotest possibility that in my future I would be kept from further hurt, pain, injustice or any such evil, I would take it. Wouldn't you?

But I don't think this is a good translation of what Jabez actually prayed for, because if God did answer this prayer for Jabez and kept him from evil or harm, it doesn't seem to me that He has answered it for anyone else before or since. Through the history of the Bible and history in general, every person, including those who fervently followed God, have suffered from the consequences of evil and experienced the pain and suffering it has brought.

If God was to bring this about for anyone, surely it would have been for Jesus, His beloved Son. But we know Jesus was mistreated, unjustly accused and as the result of the evil imposed upon Him suffered the most horrific of tortures and humiliating of deaths.

So, I don't think this idea that God *"would keep me from evil"* is the best interpretation of this phrase.

To understand this aspect of the prayer of Jabez, we need to understand that the language that describes Jabez' life and which is contained in his prayer is that of a craftsman, in particular one who is a carver by trade. One practiced in the art of shaping stone or wood.

The word for 'pain', used by Jabez' mother, the term 'keep' used in his prayer and the latter word for 'pain', all carry the connotation of shaping or fashioning in the original language.

The word pain, used by Jabez's mother to name him, is not the common word used for pain or sorrow. But, as we have said previously, it is a word referring to the carving of an idol or that pain which carves and shapes a person both physically and mentally.

The Hebrew word translated *'keep'* is the term *'āśâ*, which means to make, to work, to produce. It is the word used repeatedly in the early chapters of Genesis as well as many other places in Scripture.

Genesis 1:1 says: *"In the beginning God created"* - bārā'. 'Bara' refers to that which God creates, shapes or fashions and as stated in Hebrews 11:3 it is created from the unseen, from that which was not visible.

Hebrews 11:3 New American Standard Bible (NASB)
"By faith we understand that the world has been created by the word of God so that what is seen has not been made out of things that are visible."

But after this, the Genesis record repeatedly uses the term *āśâ* which means 'made' or 'to make from' or 'to make out of'. God made the sun, moon and stars, the land, the birds, fish and animals and then He made man in His own image and likeness. (Genesis 1:7,11, 12, 16, 25, 26, 31; 2:2, 3, 4, 18; 3:1, 7, 13 etc.)

It seems that *āśâ* refers primarily to the making or the bringing forth of something out of that which already exists. It is the transformation, the metamorphosis of the lesser reality into the greater form that it has the potential to become by the work of the hand of God.

It pictures God taking the gasses of space and rolling them in His hands and making the sun and the stars. He gathers a handful of space dust and shapes it with His hand and makes the moon, the planets. Then He takes a billion tiny grains of dust from the ground and intricately forms man.

And here in the prayer, Jabez pictures God as taking hold of his life and transforming it by the work of His hand from what it is, from that which it had become, into that which it has the potential to be.

I think that was what Jabez was praying for here, '*and may it come to pass by Your hand with me that You will make me out from this evil without shaping me with the way of pain.*'

The latter word for 'pain' is not primarily a request to be freed from the pain of the past, although that might occur through the process of his transformation. But, that God would reshape Jabez's life from that which it had become to that which only God could make it, but in doing so God would not use the way of pain or the process of pain that had shaped Jabez life in the past, to bring about His purposes.

Psalm 139:23-24 New King James Version (NKJV)
"*Search me, O God, and know my heart;*
Try me, and know my anxieties;
And see if there is any wicked way in me,
And lead me in the way everlasting.'"

The word 'wicked' is the exact same term used for 'pain' in the prayer of Jabez. So this phrase may be interpreted as '*see if there is any way of pain in me*'. Jabez is asking God to not shape his life by the way of pain as it had been in the past. It also suggests that his desire is to not use his pain or hurt to shape or influence those around him.

There was within Jabez the recognition that he had, through the process of his birth and upbringing become the product of his environment, but there existed the potential and the possibility that by the hand of God he could transcend this reality and be transformed into more than who or what he was and more than that which he and others thought he could be and this is the type of prayer that God delights in answering, because transformation is His declared purpose for every life.

God transformed Jabez's life and this is the possibility that exists for each of us. We are all to some degree the products of our environment and upbringing, and from that, for better or worse, we have made choices, decisions, that have further shaped us and determined our person and destiny. We have all to some degree been formed and shaped by evil. We have all experienced injustice and injury. We have been hurt and suffered pain and sorrow. We all carry some measure of shame, guilt and regret. We often live with degrees of anger, resentment and bitterness. We wish, like Jabez, that life's troubles, its tragedies and traumas had not happened and that they had not left their mark upon us, but, in truth, they have.

Whatever the case, evil has touched us all and the way of pain has shaped us and we all exist with the realization that because of this we are not all we could be or should be. I don't know of anyone who is truly self aware, that does not feel at times a certain deep seated sense of inadequacy and does not truly know that they are somehow less than the best possible version of themself. Each of us lives with an acute awareness that there is the potential and the possibility to be more than what I am at this moment in time.

And so Jabez recognizing who he had become because of his past, asks that God would make out from this evil or affliction to that which he could yet be. Jabez was asking God to transform his life from what is and who he had become into that which only the hand of God could make him.

When Jabez prayed *'that your hand may be with me'* it is followed by a term in Hebrew that is not generally translated into English. It is the Hebrew conjunction, *''im'* (eem). It means that which follows is directly linked to that which precedes it. In other words: *'that You will make me out from this evil and shape me without the way of pain.',* is directly attributed to the outcome of; *'and may it come to pass by Your hand with me'.*

The hand of God is not a reference to, let's say, the raw power of God, but as indicated above, the creative hand of God.

The hand creates what the heart conceives.

Beyond our words, our hands are the primary instruments that bring to reality that which we conceive in our hearts. The carver takes the raw material and sees within it the possibility of what it could be and with the skill of his hands he makes out of that which is that which he desires it to be. He sees the gnarled and knotted piece of wood and transforms it into a thing of beauty and purpose.

Jabez is saying, from his understanding, that this level of transformation is only possible by the hand of God. There is no other force, power or god that can accomplish what he is asking for. If this is to be a possibility for his life, then He has to rely completely on God and surrender his life under the hand of God because only God has the vision, the skill, the power to so radically and completely transform a life.

When he requested the hand of God to be with him, he also understood and was not asking that God would somehow change the circumstances of the past, nor does he expect the hand of God to create or control all of life's circumstances, now or in the future. In Scripture the hand of God is not portrayed as somehow eradicating the past, making it as though it never existed nor is He pictured as creating nor totally controlling the things that will come your way in the future and if you have that expectation or live with that belief you are going to be extremely disappointed with God.

What God's hand does is work every circumstance regardless of its nature, its intent towards good or evil, toward the end of His heart's desire and purpose for your life.

The hand of the carver is not seen as creating the wood or stone he works with but he takes what is and he sees within it what it can be and with every stroke of his hand carefully and meticulously crafts from what is into that image He desires and the form that makes it fits for purpose.

1 Corinthians 2:9 New International Version (NIV)
"However, as it is written:
'What no eye has seen,
what no ear has heard,
and what no human mind has conceived'—
the things God has prepared for those who love Him"

No person, not you yourself nor those who love you the most and seek the very best for your life can see or ever fully conceive of the true potential inherent within you. There is only One who knows you as you are, yet sees what you can be and has a plan to transform you into that image and fit you for His purposes.

Out of every circumstance, out of every situation God can produce in you and through you those outcomes that shape you, transform you, into the person you can be and work out His plans and purpose for your life.

That well known verse so often quoted in this context is translated two different ways:

Romans 8:28 New King James Version (NKJV)
"And we know that all things work together for good to those who love God, to those who are the called according to His purpose."

Romans 8:28 New International Version (NIV)
"And we know that in all things God works for the good of those who love him, who have been called according to his purpose."

God did not and does not create or predetermine every circumstance of your life but when your life is surrendered under His hand He will work in you and through you to make everything that comes your way produce in you the person you are capable of becoming, the person He desires you to be.

This is perhaps nowhere better illustrated than in the life of Joseph portrayed in Genesis chapters 37-50

A young man, 17 years of age, rejected and betrayed by his brothers, enslaved, imprisoned, harshly and unjustly treated over thirteen years from the age of 17 to 30. Then a further nine years later after not seeing his family for 22 years stands face to face with those who betrayed him and sold him into slavery and looks them in the eye and say from a pure heart:

Genesis 50:20 New King James Version (NKJV)
"But as for you, you meant evil against me; but God meant it for good, in order to bring it about as it is this day, to save many people alive."

It is only the hand of God that can produce that kind of outcome in the life of one who has experienced so much evil against them and endured so much pain and hurt.

Who you become and what you do will always be a direct result of the hand that makes you, the hand that shapes you.

We have all known the hurt and suffered the pain of past evil. Many have experienced the relentless suffering, anger, bitterness and resentment that comes from evil and the way of pain. You live, with every other person, with the realization that you should be and you could be more than what you are at this moment.

The message of Jabez life and prayer is that you don't have to remain trapped and determined by the evils of your past. There is an opportunity at this moment, to do as Jabez did and ask that the hand of God might be with you and that He would begin to make you from that evil and grant you a life without the way of pain shaping you.

This transformation is not the process of a moment, or a week or a month. It is the process of a lifetime.

Many of you have begun this journey, you understand the truth, that *"I am what I am by the grace of God"*, (1 Corinthians 15:10). His hand has begun to transform your life but the truth also exists that *"it does not yet appear what we shall be"* (1 John 3:2).

So wherever we are in this journey we have this assurance in of the words of the Apostle Paul in:

Philippians 1:6 New Living Translation (NLT)
*"I am certain that God, who began the good work within you,
will continue His work until it is finally finished."*

Wherever you are in this journey of transformation, God has not finished with you yet. You are not yet all you can be or will be.

I am not an advocate of simply reciting Biblical passages, like they are some magic formula, or praying a prayer by rote but right now, following an example of what has worked in transforming a life from the hurt and pain of an evil past may not be that bad of an idea.

You may never have prayed to God in your life. You may never have asked God to be the One who shapes the person you become and to fit you for the purpose your life was intended to fulfill.

You may be struggling to see that transformation taking place because all you can see and feel is the evil and pain of the past.

You may have begun the journey, but have not been as committed to the process of change as you know you should have or you simply realize that there is still more, much more that has to take place for you to become who you are capable of being.

Whatever the case, I am asking you to take this opportunity at this moment. To pray as Jabez prayed:

The prayer of Jabez:

And may it come to pass by Your hand that evil and its way of pain may not be that which shapes me. But by Your hand, You and only You will make me from that which I am into who I can yet be.

And it is my prayer that the hand of God may never lift from your life or mine and that He will continually shape you into all that His heart has purposed and all that His hand makes possible.

Ephesians 3:20 Living Bible (TLB)

"Now glory be to God, who by His mighty power at work within us is able to do far more than we would ever dare to ask or even dream of—infinitely beyond our highest prayers, desires, thoughts, or hopes."

CHAPTER 9

PRAYER IS NOT THE ANSWER

*Prayer is not the instant gratification of our wants, needs or desires,
it is the petition for the reality of a life that only God can give.*

January 2023: I was sitting in bed late at night reviewing some content I was to share the next day and I began to scan through my files of short pieces I had previously written. When I am writing, if I have a thought on some aspect of my work, I will often write it down with a brief paragraph of the idea surrounding that thought and file it for future reference. I will then, from time to time, skim back through these files to see if any of these ideas have relevance to my current line of thinking or can advance a new line of thought.

Anyway, as I was doing this I came across a file I had not opened since I wrote it in April of 2020. The first line immediately captured my attention and I thought this is the perfect opening for the last part of the prayer:

1 Chronicles 4:10
"… and to bring it into being God (granted) that which he asked for."

I had known for a long time there was a truth, a message in this line, but had never been able to encapsulate it. So this spark of inspiration some three years earlier led me to this.

The first line I wrote was:

Prayer does not change anything.

Now I know many people will recoil at this statement and may even stop reading or listening because of it. For many this statement borders on the blasphemous. But I would urge you to stay with me for a minute and let me explain. While many may disagree with me, we have all prayed prayers just like Jabez's prayer, 'God, If only this would happen.' 'If only You would do this for me.' and nothing has happened. I know people who have prayed faithfully for many years and yet nothing seems to have changed.

When Jabez prayed this prayer he was calling out for change. The tone of the first words of his prayer indicate that he was crying out in utter desperation for God to intervene in his life. But, when Jabez woke up the next morning after praying this prayer, nothing had changed. He was still surrounded by the same people. Still in the same circumstances, suffering the same pain. He didn't go to sleep in a shack and wake up in a mansion. He wasn't different in that he was suddenly more popular or had a greater level of self esteem and self confidence, where what he or others thought or had said about him no longer mattered. He wasn't miraculously emotionally healed, healthy and happy. The baggage that haunted his life yesterday was still a reality when he rolled out of bed and walked out the door to face another day.

The reality is we have all prayed prayers, had dreams and desires and no matter how we have expressed them nothing has changed. The reality is prayer doesn't change anything!

But that was only the first statement in my line of thought. The next thing I wrote and the truth is: Prayer doesn't change anything, but answered prayer changes everything.

That is the full line I had written:

Prayer doesn't change anything,
But answered prayer changes everything.

As we look at this depiction of the life of Jabez, there is an interesting word that occurs twice. It is the Hebrew word *'haya'* and it means, 'to come to pass'. The first words of the account of Jabez are *'And it came to pass'* (which not a single English translation includes in its translation) and in the middle of the prayer Jabez asks, that those things he is praying for, *'might come to pass'* by the hand of God.

What this is telling us is that there are some truths or facts we need to understand about life:

- There are things that come to pass or happen as a result of, let's say, natural circumstances. The circumstances surrounding Jabez birth, upbringing and early life were what they were. They were his unique experiences. Where you are born, who your parents are, things that transpire in life are not always of your choosing or the way you want them to be, but they are things that have come to pass.

- Then there are things that come to pass by the intervention of the hand of God in a life. Jabez as a person was transformed. Who he became and what he did were dramatically altered by the invention of God in His life. The man who *'was honored more than his breth-*

ren' was the result not of his circumstance but the result of that which came to pass by the hand of God.

His prayer was what he desired to come to pass as a result of the declared promises and purposes of God. Who he became was the result of what came to pass by the hand of God when he prayed and God answered his prayer. But to answer his prayer it says, using a different word, 'bô" - the Hebrew reads *"to bring it into being, God granted what he asked for."*

Now this term 'to bring it into being' could be equally translated 'to bring it to pass'. They have the same inherent meaning. I think the writer simply used a different term for the same reason we do, so he was not constantly repeating himself.

This means that what happened, what transpired in Jabez life was not simply the result of natural circumstance nor of his fervent desire but by the direct and intentional will and work of God.

Jabez asked and God answered. While Jabez prayer articulated the desires of his heart, that of itself did not change his life nor his circumstance. But when God answered, when God began to bring things into being on Jabez' behalf in response to his prayer, everything began to change.

The truth is there are more answers to prayer that come as a process of time than as a momentary miracle.

There are some prayers that God answers for you and some prayers God answers through you.

The miracle you are praying for, unfortunately, is often not a matter of just asking and receiving. The philosophy of name it and claim it may work on rare occasions, but in the vast majority of prayers it seems more like, ask and wait to see.

Now the issue is not in our asking God for things nor even in asking God for the wrong things.

If many of the theologians and religious critics of today had been around when Jabez prayed this prayer they would have told him that his prayer was selfish, self-centered and that it is not the kind of prayer God listens to or answers. I mean everything he asks for was for or about himself. He was praying: bless me and increase my property portfolio, and please deal with all these issues in my life, so I can be freed from my pain, my burdens and have a better life. That, in one sense, is the essence of Jabez's prayer. But God did not ignore Jabez or reprimand him for his request, He granted Him what he asked for.

I am sure most of us could come up with a list as long as our arm of the things we want, need or desire. Some of you might already have that list and be bold enough to ask God for it all. After all the Bible does say:

James 4:2 New International Version (NIV)
"You desire but do not have … You do not have, because you do not ask God. "

Or Jesus own words:

Matthew 7:7-11 New International Version (NIV)
"Ask and it will be given to you; seek and you will find; knock and the door will be opened to you. 8 For everyone who asks receives; the one who seeks finds; and to the one who knocks, the door will be opened. 9 "Which of you, if your son asks for bread, will give him a stone? 10 Or if he asks for a fish, will give him a snake? 11 If you, then, though you are evil, know how to give good gifts to your children, how much more will your Father in heaven give good gifts to those who ask Him!"

God is not anxious or worried about you asking Him for what you need, want or desire. God actually says, don't worry about issues, even about what you should ask Me for.

God, like a good parent, knows how to turn something that may not be good for you into something you can have. Anyone who is a parent and desires to be a good parent, knows you don't scold a child everytime they ask for something. And you know that children have this habit of asking for things, let's say, that are not the best option for their wellbeing. Again, you don't always ignore them or constantly tell them to stop asking, (I know we do that at times), but a good parent knows how to turn it around and satisfy the child with something that is far more beneficial. Is God any less loving or caring?

The issue is not in God's ability or willingness to answer our prayers.

"And to bring it into being God granted him that which he asked"

Ephesians 3:20 Living Bible (TLB)
*"Now glory be to God, who by His mighty power at work within us **is able** to do far more than we would ever dare to ask or even dream of* (Think about this - able to do far more than what you would even dare or be game enough to ask for. Able to do far more than what you could even dream of) *—infinitely beyond our highest prayers, desires, thoughts, or hopes."*

God is not limited in His ability or willingness to answer your prayers.

In this prayer of Jabez: It is not his ability to ask for what he wants nor is it God's ability to answer His prayer that is in question. It is the reality of what lies between those two things that we need to consider.

Between the asking: *"And Jabez called on the God of Israel ... "* and the answer: *"God granted him that which he asked for"*, there are things that God has *"to bring into being"*.

Jabez asks and God answers with the intent to bring into being that which was necessary for Jabez's prayer to become an experiential reality. We need to understand and embrace that the answer to some of our prayers is that certain things have to change, some things have yet to come into being for us to receive experientially that which we ask for.

The question we need to ask to see the answers to our prayers is: God, what is it that has to come to pass, what is it that has to come into being for me to experience the fullness of what I want and what you are willing to give me in this life?

This is the part of life and prayer we tend to struggle with the most. Between the promise and the provision there are things that have to come to pass for us to receive what we have asked for and what God grants us.

We often put these things down to the timing of God. But one of the great lessons from Israel's history is that this 'timing' issue is not as much about God delaying or waiting for the right time to give them what He had promised but it has to do with our willingness or ability to enter into and possess all that God was granting them.

Oh, I know we want it, we desire it, we pray for it. But it wasn't because the timing wasn't right that Israel wandered for forty years in the desert. God was ready to give them the land when they came to Kadesh-Barnea. It was because they were not prepared for what it would take to inherit the promise of God that they did not receive it. So God in His gracious anger did not take them into a place where, He knew, they would be defeated and destroyed by their own fears and failures. He had to bring into being a people who were possessed of a different spirit before they could possess the promise and enter the land.

The delays experienced in our receiving the fullness of what we want and what God willingly gifts us is, from a Biblical perspective, more about our preparedness to enter and to live in the fullness of that promise and its provision than it is an issue of timing.

There is an incredible statement found in:

2 Peter 3:9 New International Version (NIV)
*"The Lord is not slow in keeping His promise, as some understand
slowness. Instead He is patient with you, **not wanting**
anyone to perish, but everyone to come to repentance."*

The answer to God's timing in bringing to pass what He has purposed and promised has far less to do with what we want, or God's willingness to grant our requests, it has to do with what He is NOT wanting to happen.

And from the Biblical, Divine perspective there are two things God does not want to happen.

As we just said, when Israel first came to the edge of the Promised Land they were not prepared to enter into the provision of that promise. What if you are asking God for something that He knows you are not prepared for? What if the delay to your prayer is because God does NOT WANT you to receive it and lose it because you are not ready to fully embrace it? What if there are things God needs to bring into being, within you, so you can not only receive it but continue to live in the blessing and fullness of the promise.

We would like to think everything God gifts us is unconditional, but that is not always the case. It takes faith and courage to step into some of those things you seek. It takes commitment and obedience and wisdom to live in the fullness of God's provision. Even when Israel entered the land, they encountered opposition and they eventually lost possession of the land because they were unwilling to pay the price to continue to walk in that blessing.

There are consequences to our failures.

What God is not wanting is for you to enter His promise and then lose it because you are not prepared to pay the price or maintain the commitments to live and fully possess all that He is giving you.

Jabez prayed for three things: Blessing, increased territory, and deep personal change. (Pretty much a simple bucket list of requirements for a happy, successful, fulfilled life).

But:

- The price of blessing is obedience.
- The price of increased territory is more responsibility.
- The price of change is being teachable and disciplined.

To ask for blessing is simple and it's not hard for God to bless you. In fact it is His declared desire to bless you. But to bring it into being, for you to walk in and live in the blessing of God, that requires obedience. Deuteronomy 28 teaches us that. But, obedience, for me, is a challenge. My observation is people are willing to be obedient in a crisis but the more comfortable we become the more optional our commitment to obedience is. The more leeway we give ourselves to be flexible with our commitment to God and His ways.

But failure to walk in obedience is to walk in the way of the curse, to experience the way of pain and to forfeit the blessing of God.

To ask for increase is not a problem. Our desire for more, for increase in almost every area of life is natural. To seek to grow, to seek an education, to seek for a job, to seek for a promotion, to seek for a life partner, a family, a home, financial security, there is nothing inherently wrong or selfish about any of these things. We could define the desire for them in God's original decree of blessing over mankind. *'Be fruitful and multiply'* (Genesis 1:28). For God to enlarge, to bring increase in almost every area of your life is something He is more than willing to do. But to receive it and to walk in it requires that you be prepared for and be able to handle greater levels of responsibility. Most of us want more. But more responsibility? More of the pressure and subsequent drama that comes with that responsibility. I don't think so. We want the benefits but we don't want to pay the price.

To fail to accept the responsibility of following God and honoring His ways will result in the devourer and the way of pain.

God, I want change, real change. Do you? Are you eager or even willing to embrace new ways of thinking and new ways of doing things and forming the new habits and the discipline it takes for real change to happen. For many, even the suggestion of change is greeted with, 'But we have never done it that way before'.

The idea of change for most people involves either a miraculous change in our circumstance or for the other person to have an attitude adjustment or in some cases a total personality transplant. When we talk about wanting change. We want our circumstances to change. We want other people to change. But to embrace change, change in ourselves. Me? Change? The only way you are going to get from where you are to where you want to be is to embrace something new, which is what change is. If you cannot or will not embrace change the consequence is the way of pain.

If you ask, God will answer and deliver you from the hand of evil and the way of pain.

But the reason God is slow at times is not because of what you want nor His willingness to give you what you want but because of what He is **not wanting** to come to pass.

God is patient, not because He expects you to fail, but because He so desperately wants you to succeed. And not to return to experiencing the way of pain that you so desperately want not to shape your life.

He wants you to have the good things, Those things that you desire and dream of, hope for and pray for. God is not withholding them from you.

All the promises of God are 'yes' and 'amen' in Christ Jesus, (2 Corinthians 1:20). God says yes and we confirm it with a fist pumping amen. But He is wanting to give you the best opportunity to hold on to, to possess, to walk in, to live in the fullness of that which He provides. God does not have a problem giving good gifts to His children. But it breaks His heart to see His children, being robbed of and losing that which He has so generously given. And we lose it not simply because there are things that take it from us but that we were not prepared to be obedient, responsible and disciplined enough to walk in the fullness of it.

Jabez, was granted that which he asked for and by all accounts He continued in the blessing and the increase of it all the days of His life. Never wavering in His commitment to follow God to that point where he is recorded as being honored more than all his peers.

The challenges to our life and our desire to live out our faith are real. Some may decry the power of prayer. Those who have had God answer their prayers know the reality of the power and goodness of God, not in theory but in experience.

Perhaps my line is true. Prayer doesn't just change anything. But answered prayer changes everything.

Philippians 4:6 New International Version (NIV)
"Do not be anxious about anything, (not even what you are asking God for)*, but in every situation, by prayer and petition, with thanksgiving, present your requests to God."*

Don't stop asking God for the good things you desire.

Don't stop believing that God is wanting and willing to grant you what you ask for.

But I would also encourage you, in the midst of your prayer, to ask: What has to come to pass? What is it God, You have to bring into being for me to experience the fullness of what I am asking God for?

Ephesians 3:20 Living Bible (TLB)
"Now glory be to God, who by His mighty power at work within us is able to do far more than we would ever dare to ask or even dream of—infinitely beyond our highest prayers, desires, thoughts, or hopes."

CHAPTER 10

THE LEGACY

*Your legacy is not just what you do in your lifetime but what you achieve
that those in the generations that follow can walk in and build upon.*

Jabez was an ordinary man who rose from obscurity through circumstances that were far from ideal and made his life count for something. He made his mark in his generation and created a legacy for the ages.

I believe deep down most of us want our lives to do the same. We want to do something that matters and makes a difference. We want more than just our name in the Registry of Births, Deaths and Marriages to show that we once existed. We want to achieve a level of significance, not because of ego, but because of a belief that every life was created to have purpose, meaning and significance. So, why is it that some rise to a level of influence and impact where so many don't?

The opening line of the record of Jabez life says:

"And it came to pass, Jabez was honored more than his brethren."

This means he was held in high esteem and greatly respected, even revered by those who knew him. It means he achieved something during his lifetime that made him standout from the crowd and become worthy of a level of recognition that was greater than almost any other in his day. He received this honor because of who he became and because of what he did.

The curiosity is, his name is remembered but his achievements are not recorded.

So the question becomes: Why would you remember a person, honoring their name and yet record nothing of their achievements? There is not even a hint within this biography of anything that Jabez did, except for his prayer. It is as if the reader is expected to know just by the mention of his name what he had done, even in the centuries following his passing.

There are few people in history that have ever achieved this level of honor and recognition, where their name alone is all you need in order to know something of what they did. In the Biblical context there are many renowned characters, but in the broader context of the anals of history this kind of esteem is reserved for Moses and Jesus and sometimes the Apostle Paul. These alone are those included in the extended list of influential people. Other high profile historical figures listed as people of renown include: Napoleon, Muhammad, William Shakespeare, Abraham Lincoln, George Washington, Adolf Hitler, Aristotle.[4] While this list can be greatly expanded and argued about, my point is that many of us would at least know something of these people's 'achievements' by the mention of their name.

But the question I really want to answer is: What did Jabez do that made him worthy of such honor?

Jabez is honored in a twofold manner:

---

[4] https://www.theguardian.com/books/2014/jan/30/whos-most-significant-historical-figure

Firstly, He is honored by God, in that his prayer was such that it was deemed worthy to be honored by granting that which he asked. Even though the prayer was very personal in what Jabez asked for, it was not deemed to be a selfish, self-centered or an egotistical request. One marked by pride or selfish ambition. If it is marked by anything, it is the humility of the broken.

Psalm 51:17 New King James Version (NKJV)
"The sacrifices of God are a broken spirit,
A broken and a contrite heart—
These, O God, You will not despise."

God honored Jabez by answering his prayer and transforming his life.

Secondly, he is honored in that his name is recorded in the pages of history in the greatest book that has ever been written. Of all the people that had lived and could have been chosen to be honored from within these genealogies, which includes kings, leaders of tribes, heads of clans and families, Jabez is honored in a way that no other is within the context of these nine chapters. Even the greatest of them is mentioned only in name, but Jabez 'life is described, even if only briefly within these pages. Though he is not mentioned in the other records of Israel's history, the author of this text could not bypass Jabez with just the mention of his name. To honor him was to at least tell his story.

To have your name remembered among those who are contained in these lists is no small honor. Jabez is mentioned by name only four times in the Bible, all in 1 Chronicles. Three times in 1 Chronicles 4:9-10 and once in 1 Chronicles 2:55 where it is recorded as the name of a village in Israel.

1 Chronicles 2:55 New International Version (NIV)
"and the clans of scribes who lived at Jabez: the Tirathites,
Shimeathites and Sucathites. These are the Kenites who
came from Hammath, the father of the Rekabites."

I want you to notice that the phrase, *'who lived at Jabez'* makes no difference to the reading of this passage or the reference to these people. Read this passage without these words and it still makes sense and conveys the relevant information. We are not even sure of the precise location of this village, except that it was within the bounds of the territory allocated to the tribe of Judah. If it were omitted from the text it would make almost no difference to our understanding of who these people were and what they did. It seems to me that the only reason it was included was to establish a connection between these scribes and the person this town is named after.

That the town itself is called Jabez is not likely random. Towns often bore the name of their founder or were changed to reflect the one who possessed it through conquest.

Jabez was either the village that Jabez possessed and renamed in answer to his prayer that God *'would greatly increase his territory'* or one that he established within that territory. There is also the possibility that this town was renamed at some later date to honor his memory and to carry on his legacy because it carried on the traditions for which he had become renowned.

Much like we do today when we name a stadium or one of its stands in honor of some famous sports star or a theater after a famed performer or a lecture hall or university building after one of its notable alumni. But it would be highly unusual to name a sports stand after, say, a famed opera singer. There is a connection between the person, the place where they are honored and what they did.

Jabez, the town, seems to point toward the legacy of Jabez, the person, and that for which he was honored.

As well as this reference in Scripture, Jewish tradition records Jabez as a great and revered teacher of the Law of Moses. He is said to have traveled throughout Israel, much like Jesus did centuries later, publicly teaching the people from the Law of Moses so they would know God and follow His ways. He is said to have gathered many disciples, like the scribes linked to his name in the town of Jabez.

What is truly noteworthy is these scribes were not priests or from the nobles or ruling class. They were not even Israelites by birth, they were Kenites, the people of Midian associated with Jethro, Moses' father-in-law, a largely nomadic people. Yet these became scribes in Israel.

Why is this so outstanding? Because in ancient times, literacy, the ability to read and write was a privilege generally reserved for the elite. It is estimated that in ancient times that even among the most developed nations literacy was probably less than 5% of the population. So this record of common people being educated to what we would call a standard of 'higher education', far beyond that of the teaching of oral traditions passed from the father to his family through stories, songs and poems, which was the education of the average person, is noteworthy, to say the least.

Jabez through his prayer and in his commitment to God experienced the power of truth, that the word of God was transformative and he began to teach others what he had experienced. He continued to learn and teach to the point where tradition says He was considered and esteemed as a great teacher in Israel.

Jabez is honored as perhaps the first great scribe and teacher of the Law among the people after Moses and Joshua.

His legacy is in the scribes and the scribal traditions that were established in his name.

As I just said, these scribes mentioned here were not nobles and rulers of the land, they were not even Israelites by birth. But for these people to become scribes means that there was a system of education established where people learned to read and write. There was a system where people were taught the Law of God. The scribes wrote legal documents. They were the academics and lawyers of their day. Some recorded the history of their time, some of which we now know as the Bible. They were, within Israel, teachers of the Law of God. They taught the principles and truths of the Law. They taught the people to know God and to walk in His ways. They also made meticulous handwritten copies of the Law and their history and preserved it over the centuries.

A time would come when the nation of Israel would collapse, Jerusalem and the magnificent Temple of Solomon would be destroyed. The people would be captives and go into exile. Much of their history and traditions would be lost.

Seventy years after the destruction of Jerusalem, King Cyrus of Persia decreed that the Jews could return to their land and rebuild their Temple. One of those who returned and in fact led the rebuilding of the Temple and later stood alongside Nehemiah in the rebuilding of the city was a priest and scribe named Ezra. He would have been born and raised in captivity, having never seen the Temple nor the city. Yet He was a scribe, an expert in the Law of God. He taught the people who returned to know God and to honor His Word.

Nehemiah 8:5-8 New International Version (NIV)
"Ezra opened the book. All the people could see him because he was
standing above them; and as he opened it, the people all stood up. ...
7 The Levites ... instructed the people in the Law while the people were
standing there. 8 They read from the Book of the Law of God, making it clear
and giving the meaning so that the people understood what was being read."

The amazing thing is that the Word of God survived and copies were made through the captivity. People were educated and taught to know God and honor God while in exile. Ezra was one of those who emerged as a leader and teacher of his people. He is credited with the establishing a school in Jerusalem for the underprivileged, for boys who had lost their father and therefore had lost the one who traditionally would teach them as a daily routine in the home by word of mouth and by personal example show them what it was to know God, follow God and to walk in His ways.

Ezra, like many who rise in the ranks of their profession, know and honor their history and its traditions. Ezra is the scribe that is credited with recording and honoring the life of Jabez. He is credited with the writing of the Book of Chronicles, which was originally a single work including l & ll Chronicles as well as the Books of Ezra and Nehemiah. It was Ezra who walked the path of the one who went before him, who could not and did not allow the name and the memory of this man to disappear from history and who in turn carried his legacy into a whole new era.

The tradition of the scribes was reestablished. The word of God was transcribed and translated into other languages so people of every tribe, tongue and nation might have the opportunity to know God and hear of His great works.

This legacy and these traditions stand to this day. As of 2022 all of the Bible has been translated into 724 languages, the New Testament has been translated into an additional 1,617 languages, and smaller portions of the Bible have been translated into 1,248 other languages according to Wycliffe Global Alliance.[5] We have those who dedicate their lives to teaching, transcribing and translating the Word of God so that all people might hear the message in their native tongue, that they might hear of God's great and mighty works, come to know Him and have their lives transformed by His amazing grace.

We have the Word of God, along with its history and traditions that have been preserved and passed down generation after generation because of a practice somehow associated with the life and legacy of Jabez.

Jabez honor lay not in fame or fortune. He did not win wars, build cities or empires. There are no great monuments that bear his image or name. But his legacy is people. People who came to know God, who held onto God and the truth of His Word and presented it and preserved it through the rise and fall of nations and of the empires that would come and go in the course of history. The values and traditions associated with his name have held fast in every generation from then till now. Because of it, literally billions of lives have been transformed across the generations that have followed.

His life resounds in the words of Daniel the Prophet

Daniel 11:32-33 New King James Version (NKJV)
"But the people who know their God shall be strong, and carry out great exploits. 33 And those of the people who understand shall instruct many."

Jabez is not a man that world history records as great and it does not even know his name. But however it happened, we have this man whose life and legacy is associated with the proclamation and preservation of the

---

[5]   https://en.wikipedia.org/wiki/Bible_translations

Word of God. One, who not only influenced people during his lifetime, but through time and into eternity. One who did not remain in the confines of the boundaries life had set but reached beyond himself and even his own culture to teach a foreign people to know God and honor His Word. He, indeed, is worthy of the highest of honor.

Our legacy is not formed after we die but it is the culmination of what we stand for and achieved in our lifetime. It is forged in what you do today, tomorrow and the years that lie ahead. And to me, there can be no greater honor, no greater legacy than that of seeing lives transformed by the Word of God and the grace of God. That someone like Jabez, living in pain, seeking answers, real answers to life's questions, came to know the goodness and mercy of God and be transformed and reshape their life to become the person they never thought possible and then in turn used their gifts and knowledge to help transform the lives of those around them, to be honored more than them all, because he knew a:

Ephesians 3:20 Living Bible (TLB)
"God, who by His mighty power at work within us is able to do far more than we would ever dare to ask or even dream of—infinitely beyond our highest prayers, desires, thoughts, or hopes."

APPENDIX A

HEBREW TEXT ANALYSIS

1 Chronicles 4:9-10:

(transliterated from the Hebrew of the Masoretic Text)

"Now it came to pass, Jabez was honored more than his brethren and his mother called his name Jabez saying, 'because I brought forth in pain'. And Jabez called to Elohim (the God) of Israel saying, 'If only with blessing will You continue to bless me and will You greatly increase my territory and may it come to pass by Your hand with me that You will make me out from this evil without shaping me with the way of pain.' And to bring it into being Elohim (God) granted that which he asked for."

Below is my textual study of the Hebrew Masoretic Text transliterated into English. It should be understood that one language was not created with the idea that it would translate well into other languages and particularly those languages not derived or developed from the same or similar base.

Note1: In the text above the words underlined do not appear and are not translated from the Hebrew text; they are implied or added to give a better sense to the reading.

Note 2: You will notice some words are written after others in the Hebrew language which is the reverse of the way we speak: ie <u>W4</u> וַיָּחֶם (remember that Hebrew is read from left to right) reading 'more than brethren his' which will be translated as english 'more than his brethren'.

Note 3: Below the closest literal translated word will be listed and if a word is placed in brackets () after it, it will be the word chosen to give it the better English grammatical rendering.

Note 4: This is my understanding of the text from many hours of research. I am not a Hebrew scholar and I am more than willing to be corrected in any points of clear misinterpretation, not merely opinion.

MASORETIC TEXT
https://www.blueletterbible.org/kjv/1ch/4/1/t_conc_342009

4:9 וַיְהִי יַעְבֵּץ נִכְבָּד מֵאֶחָיו וְאִמּוֹ קָרְאָה שְׁמוֹ יַעְבֵּץ לֵאמֹר כִּי יָלַדְתִּי בְּעֹצֶב׃

4:10 וַיִּקְרָא יַעְבֵּץ לֵאלֹהֵי יִשְׂרָאֵל לֵאמֹר אִם־בָּרֵךְ תְּבָרֲכֵנִי וְהִרְבִּיתָ אֶת־גְּבוּלִי וְהָיְתָה יָדְךָ עִמִּי וְעָשִׂיתָ מֵּרָעָה לְבִלְתִּי עָצְבִּי וַיָּבֵא אֱלֹהִים אֵת אֲשֶׁר־שָׁאָל

MASORETIC TEXT
https://www.blueletterbible.org/kjv/1ch/4/1/t_conc_342009

4:9 וַיְהִי יַעְבֵּץ נִכְבָּד מֵאֶחָיו וְאִמּוֹ קָרְאָה שְׁמוֹ יַעְבֵּץ לֵאמֹר כִּי יָלַדְתִּי בְּעֹצֶב׃

SECTION:1

4:9a וַיְהִי יַעְבֵּץ מֵאֶחָיו

W1 וַיְהִי	וַ	Classical Hebrew: **wāw**; Strong's Number h9007; Speech: conjunction (https://www.blueletterbible.org/kjv/1ch/4/1/p1/ss0/t_conc_342009/=parsing/Code:C)	And (Now)
	יְהִי	Classical Hebrew: **hāyâ**; Strong's Number h1961; Speech: verb; Stem: Qal; Type: Sequential imperfect; Person: Third Person; Gender: Masculine; Number: Singular (https://www.blueletterbible.org/kjv/1ch/4/1/p1/ss0/t_conc_342009/=parsing/Code:Vqw3ms) (https://www.blueletterbible.org/lexicon/h1961/kjv/wlc/0-1/)	it came to pass

| W2 יַעְבֵּץ | Classical Hebrew: **ya bēṣ**; Strong's Number h3258; Speech: <u>Noun</u>; Type: <u>Proper Name</u> https://www.blueletterbible.org/ kjv/1ch/4/1/t_conc_342009/=parsing/ Code:Np) (https://www.blueletterbible.org/lexicon/ h3258/kjv/wlc/0-1/) In Hebrew, "Jabez" is a play on words. His mother named him from her pain. The word she used for pain was ʾōṣeḇ *'because I brought forth in pain'*. ōṣeḇ is from a primitive root **'âtsab'**; properly, to carve, i.e. fabricate or fashion. (https://www.blueletterbible.org/lexicon/ h6087/kjv/wlc/0-1/=Strong's Definitions) Then remember that there is no "J" in Hebrew. In fact, there was no "J" in any language until the 14th century. The letter is "Y," not "J." And because we don't read the text in Hebrew, we don't see the connection between "in pain" **be-ʾōṣeb** and **"Ya bêts."** (https://skipmoen.com/2021/04/ the-real-prayer-of-jabez/) | Jabez |

| W3 נִכְבָּד | Classical Hebrew: **kābad**; Strong's Number h3513; Speech: <u>verb</u>; Stem: <u>Niphal</u>; Type: <u>Participle Active</u>; Gender: <u>Masculine</u>; Number: <u>Singular</u>; State: <u>Absolute</u>

(https://www.blueletterbible.org/kjv/1ch/4/1/ p1/ss0/t_conc_342009/=parsing /Code: VNrmsa)

(https://www.blueletterbible.org/lexicon/ h3513/kjv/wlc/0-1/)

Several translations, including NASB, NIV, NKJV and RSV prefer to translate נִכְבָּד as "honorable" rather than "honored," but a survey of the other thirty occurrences of נִכְבָּד suggests that the verb normally implies esteem granted to its grammatical subject by others, rather than a personal quality abstractly attaching to the subject. "Honored" is thus preferable as a translation.

(RC Heard · 2003 · Cited by 12 — Echoes of Genesis in 1 Chronicles 4:9–10: An Intertextual and Contextual Reading of Jabez's Prayer. https://jhsonline.org/index.php/jhs/article/ view/5859) | was honored |

W4 מֵאֶחָיו	מֵ	Strong's Number h251; Speech: Preposition (https://www.blueletterbible.org/kjv/1ch/4/1/p1/ss0/t_conc_342009/=parsing/Code: R) (https://www.blueletterbible.org/lexicon/h251/kjv/wlc/0-1/) (https://en.wiktionary.org/wiki/%D7%9E%D6%BE/=Preposition 2)	more than
	אֶחָי	Classical Hebrew: 'āḥ; Strong's Number h251; Speech: Noun; Type: Common; Gender: Masculine; Number: Plural; State: Construct (https://www.blueletterbible.org/kjv/1ch/4/1/p1/ss0/t_conc_342009/=parsing/Code: Ncmpc) (https://www.blueletterbible.org/lexicon/h251/kjv/wlc/0-1/) 'âch; a primitive word; a brother (used in the widest sense of literal relationship) i.e. kindred, clan, tribe, etc. (https://www.blueletterbible.org/lexicon/h251/kjv/wlc/0-1/=Strong's Definitions)	brethren
	ו	Speech: Suffix; Type: Pronominal; Person: Third Person; Gender: Masculine; Number: Singular (https://www.blueletterbible.org/kjv/1ch/4/1/p1/ss0/t_conc_342009/=parsing/Code: Sp3ms)	his

| ו | Speech: <u>Suffix</u>; Type: <u>Pronominal</u>; Person: <u>Third Person</u>; Gender: <u>Masculine</u>; Number: <u>Singular</u>

(https://www.blueletterbible.org/kjv/1ch/4/1/ p1/ss0/t_conc_342009/=parsing/Code: Sp3ms) | his |

1 Chronicles 4:9a "Now it came to pass, Jabez was honored more than his brethren."

	SECTION: 2	

4:9b וְאִמּוֹ קָרְאָה שְׁמוֹ יַעְבֵּץ לֵאמֹר כִּי יָלַדְתִּי בְּעֹצֶב׃

W5 וְאִמּוֹ	ו	Classical Hebrew: **wāw**; Strong's Number <u>h9007</u>; Speech: <u>conjunction</u> (https://www.blueletterbible.org/kjv/1ch/4/1/t_conc_342009/=parsing/Code:C)	and
	אִמּ	Classical Hebrew: **'ēm**; Strong's Number h517; Speech: <u>Noun</u>; Type: <u>Common</u>; Gender: <u>Feminine</u>; Number: <u>Singular</u>; State: <u>Construct</u> (https://www.blueletterbible.org/kjv/1ch/4/1/t_conc_342009/=parsing/Code:Ncfsc) (https://www.blueletterbible.org/lexicon/h517/kjv/wlc/0-1/)	mother
	וֹ	Speech: <u>Suffix</u>; Type: <u>Pronominal</u>; Person: <u>Third Person</u>; Gender: <u>Masculine</u>; Number: <u>Singular</u> (https://www.blueletterbible.org/kjv/1ch/4/1/t_conc_342009/=parsing/Code Sp3ms)	his

W6 קָרְאָה		Classical Hebrew: **qārā'** Strong's Number h7121;; Speech: <u>verb</u>; Stem: <u>Qal</u>; Type: <u>Perfect (qatal)</u>; Person: <u>Third Person</u> Gender: <u>Feminine</u>; Number: <u>Singular</u> (https://www.blueletterbible.org/kjv/1ch/4/1/t_conc_342009/=parsing/Code:Vqp3fs) (https://www.blueletterbible.org/lexicon/h7121/kjv/wlc/0-1/)	called
W7 שְׁמוֹ	שֵׁם	Classical Hebrew: **šēm**; Strong's Number h8034; Speech: <u>Noun</u>; Type: <u>Common</u>; Gender: <u>Masculine</u>; Number: <u>Singular</u>; State: <u>Construct</u> (https://www.blueletterbible.org/lexicon/h8034/kjv/wlc/0-1//=parsing/Code:Ncmsc) (https://www.blueletterbible.org/lexicon/h8034/kjv/wlc/0-1/)	name
	וֹ	Speech: <u>Suffix</u>; Type: <u>Pronominal</u>; Person: <u>Third Person</u>; Gender: <u>Masculine</u>; Number: <u>Singular</u> (https://www.blueletterbible.org/lexicon/h8034/kjv/wlc/0-1/=parsing/Code:Sp3ms)	his
W8 יַעְבֵּץ		See 'Jabez' <u>W2</u> above.	Jabez

W9 לֵאמֹר	לְ	Strong's Number h9009; Speech: Preposition (https://www.blueletterbible.org/kjv/1ch/4/1/t_conc_3420091/=parsing/Code:R) Both Biblical Hebrew and Biblical Aramaic have four primary prepositions: the prefix בְּ (in, at, by); the prefix לְ (to, for); the prefix כְּ (as, like); and the prefix מִ (which is a shortened form of the independent preposition מִן, meaning "from"). (https://uhg.readthedocs.io/en/latest/preposition.html#:~:text=Both%20Biblical%20Hebrew%20and%20Biblical,a%20family%20of%20other%20prepositions.)	to
	אמֹר	Classical Hebrew: **ʾāmar**; Strong's Number h559; Speech: verb; Stem: Qal; Type: Infinitive Construct; (https://www.blueletterbible.org/kjv/1ch/4/1/t_conc_3420091/=parsing/Code:Vqc) (https://www.blueletterbible.org/lexicon/h559/kjv/wlc/0-1/)	say (saying)
W10 כִּי		Classical Hebrew: **kî**; Strong's Number h3588; Speech: conjunction (https://www.blueletterbible.org/kjv/1ch/4/1/t_conc_342009/=parsing/Code:C) (https://www.blueletterbible.org/lexicon/h3588/kjv/wlc/0-1/)	because

W11 יָלַדְתִּי		Classical Hebrew: **yālaḏ**; Strong's Number h3205; Speech: <u>verb</u>; Stem: <u>Qal</u>; Type: <u>Perfect (qatal)</u>; Person: <u>First Person</u> Gender: <u>Common</u>; Number: <u>Singular</u> https://www.blueletterbible.org/lexicon/h3205/kjv/wlc/0-1/=parsing/Code:Vqp1cs) (https://www.blueletterbible.org/lexicon/h3205/kjv/wlc/0-1/)	I brought forth
W12 בְּעֹצֶב	בְּ	Strong's Number <u>h9004</u>; Speech: <u>Preposition</u> (https://www.blueletterbible.org/kjv/1ch/4/1/t_conc_342009/=parsing/Code:R) See <u>W9</u> above	in
	עֹצֶב	Classical Hebrew: ʻōṣeḇ; Strong's Number h6090; Speech: <u>Noun</u>; Type: <u>Common</u>; Gender: <u>Masculine</u>; Number: <u>Singular</u>; State: <u>Absolute</u> https://www.blueletterbible.org/kjv/1ch/4/1/t_conc_342009/=parsing/Code:Ncmsa) ʻôtseb; a variation of H6089; an idol (as fashioned); also pain (bodily or mental) (https://www.blueletterbible.org/lexicon/h6089/kjv/wlc/0-1/=Strong's Definitions)	pain

1 Chronicles 4:9b "And his mother called his name Jabez saying, 'because I brought forth in pain'."

MASORETIC TEXT
https://www.blueletterbible.org/kjv/1ch/4/1/t_conc_342009
4:10 וַיִּקְרָא יַעְבֵּץ לֵאלֹהֵי יִשְׂרָאֵל לֵאמֹר אִם־בָּרֵךְ תְּבָרֲכֵנִי וְהִרְבִּיתָ אֶת־גְּבוּלִי וְהָיְתָה יָדְךָ עִמִּי וְעָשִׂיתָ מֵּרָעָה לְבִלְתִּי עָצְבִּי וַיָּבֵא אֱלֹהִים אֵת אֲשֶׁר־שָׁאָל

SECTION: 3

4:10a וַיִּקְרָא יַעְבֵּץ לֵאלֹהֵי יִשְׂרָאֵל לֵאמֹר

W13 וַיִּקְרָא	וְ	Classical Hebrew: **wāw**; Strong's Number h9007; Speech: conjunction https://www.blueletterbible.org/kjv/1ch/4/1/t_conc_342010/=parsing/Code:C)	And
	יִּקְרָא	Classical Hebrew: **qārā'**; Strong's Number h7121; Speech: verb; Stem: Qal; Type: Sequential imperfect; Person: Third Person Gender: Masculine; Number: Singular (https://www.blueletterbible.org/kjv/1ch/4/1/t_conc_342009/=parsing/Code:Vqp3fs) (https://www.blueletterbible.org/lexicon/h7121/kjv/wlc/0-1/)	called
W14 יַעְבֵּץ		See 'Jabez' W2 above.	Jabez

W15	לְ	Strong's Number h9004; Speech: Preposition (https://www.blueletterbible.org/kjv/1ch/4/1/t_conc_342010/=parsing/Code:R) See W9 above	to
לֵאלֹהֵי	אלֹהֵי	Classical Hebrew: 'ĕlōhîm Strong's Number h430;; Speech: Noun; Type: Common; Gender: Masculine; Number: Plural; State: Construct (https://www.blueletterbible.org/kjv/1ch/4/1/t_conc_342010/=parsing/Code:Ncmpc) (https://www.blueletterbible.org/lexicon/h430/kjv/wlc/0-1/) *El* is the generic name for God, used among a number of ancient cultures, in fact it describes any god, any deity, but God did not reveal Himself as El, a god, one among many, but by the name *Elohim.* The added *'im'* ending denotes a plural masculine noun. Through the use of plurality we have often been led to believe this is a reference to the triune nature of the Godhead - God the Father, God the Son and God the Holy Spirit - but this is not strictly the case. When used of the true God, "Elohim" denotes what is called by linguists a plural of majesty, honor, or fullness. That is, He is GOD in the fullest sense of the word. He is "GOD of gods" or literally, "ELOHIM of elohim" (Deut 10:17; Ps 136:2). Jabez did not call on a god but the Elohim of Israel, the God of all gods. (https://www.hebrew-streams.org/works/hebrew/context-elohim.html)	Elohim (the God)

W16 יִשְׂרָאֵל		Classical Hebrew: **yiśrā'ēl**; Strong's Number h3478; Speech: <u>Noun</u>; Type: <u>Proper Name</u> (https://www.blueletterbible.org/kjv/1ch/4/1/t_conc_342010/=parsing/Code:Np) (https://www.blueletterbible.org/lexicon/h3478/kjv/wlc/0-1/)	(of) Israel
W17 לֵאמֹר	לְ	Strong's Number <u>h9009</u>; Speech: <u>Preposition</u> (https://www.blueletterbible.org/kjv/1ch/4/1/t_conc_342010/=parsing/Code:R) See <u>W9</u> above	to
	אמר	Strong's Number h559; Classical Hebrew: **'āmar**; Speech: <u>verb</u>; Stem: <u>Qal</u>; Type: <u>Infinitive Construct</u> (https://www.blueletterbible.org/kjv/1ch/4/1/t_conc_3420091/=parsing/Code:Vqc) (https://www.blueletterbible.org/lexicon/h559/kjv/wlc/0-1/)	say (saying)
1 Chronicles 4:10a "And Jabez called to Elohim (the God) *of* Israel saying			

SECTION: 4			
4:10b אִם־בָּרֵךְ תְּבָרֲכֵנִי וְהִרְבִּיתָ אֶת־גְּבוּלִי			
W18 אִם־בָּרֵ	אִם	Classical Hebrew: **'im**; Strong's Number h518; Speech: conjunction (https://www.blueletterbible.org/kjv/1ch/4/1/t_conc_342010/=parsing/Code:C) (https://www.blueletterbible.org/lexicon/h518/kjv/wlc/0-1/) The opening 'im commonly means "if," but is a "particle of wishing" in contexts such as this. (The Prayer of Jabez: A Biblical-Theological Examination by Benjamin Shaw, ThM, PhD (candidate)) (https://blogs.bible.org/translating-what-isnt-there-was-the-prayer-of-jabez-a-prayer/)	If only
	בָּרֵ	Classical Hebrew: **bāraḵ**; Strong's Number h1288; Speech: verb; Stem: Piel; Type: Infinitive Absolute (https://www.blueletterbible.org/kjv/1ch/4/1/t_conc_3420091/=parsing/Code:Vpa) (https://www.blueletterbible.org/lexicon/h1288/kjv/wlc/0-1/) In the original Hebrew language there is no expression of intensity, like 'indeed', or 'greatly'. The dual use of the term conveys an intensity of desire.	with blessing

W19 תְּבָרֵךְ תְּבָרֲכֵנִי		Classical Hebrew: **bārak**; Strong's Number h1288; Speech: <u>verb</u>; Stem: <u>Piel</u>; Type: <u>Imperfect (yiqtol)</u>; Person: <u>Second Person</u> Gender: <u>Masculine</u>; Number: <u>Singular</u> (https://www.blueletterbible.org/kjv/1ch/4/1/t_conc_3420091/=parsing/Code:Vpi2ms) <u>Imperfect (yiqtol)</u>; Generally designates an action which is continuous, incomplete, or open-ended. Rather than depicting an action as a single event, the imperfect depicts it as a continuing process. (https://www.blueletterbible.org/lexicon/h1288/kjv/wlc/0-1/)	will You continue to bless
	נִי	Speech: <u>Suffix</u>; Type: <u>Pronominal</u>; Person: <u>First Person</u>; Gender: <u>Common</u>; Number: <u>Singular</u> (https://www.blueletterbible.org/kjv/1ch/4/1/t_conc_342010/=parsing/Code:Sp1cs)	me
W20 וְהִרְבִּיתָ	ו	Strong's Number h9007; Classical Hebrew: **wāw**; Speech: <u>conjunction</u> https://www.blueletterbible.org/kjv/1ch/4/1/t_conc_342010/=parsing/Code:C)	and
	הִרְבִּיתָ	Classical Hebrew: **rābâ**; Strong's Number h7235; Speech: <u>verb</u>; Stem: <u>Hiphil</u>; Type: <u>Sequential Perfect (weqatal)</u>; Person: <u>Second Person</u> Gender: <u>Masculine</u>; Number: <u>Singular</u> https://www.blueletterbible.org/kjv/1ch/4/1/t_conc_342010/=parsing/Code:Vhq2ms) (https://www.blueletterbible.org/lexicon/h7235/kjv/wlc/0-1/)	will You greatly increase

W21	אֵת	Classical Hebrew: **'eth**; Strong's Number h0853; Speech: untranslated particle	
אֶת־גְּבוּ לִי?		(http://lexiconcordance.com/hebrew/0853.html) Apparently contracted from **H0226** in the demonstrative sense of *entity*; properly *self* (but generally used to point out more definitely the object of a verb or preposition, *even* or *namely*):—(As such unrepresented in English.) (http://lexiconcordance.com/hebrew/0853.html—Brown-Driver-Briggs(Old Testament Hebrew-English Lexicon))	
	גְּבוּל	Classical Hebrew: **gᵉbûl**; Strong's Number h1366; Classical Hebrew: **gᵉbûl**; Speech: Noun; Type: Common; Gender: Masculine; Number: Singular; State: Construct (https://www.blueletterbible.org/kjv/1ch/4/1/t_conc_342010/=parsing/Code:Ncmsc) Territory (enclosed within boundary); by implication that which limits. (https://www.blueletterbible.org/lexicon/h1366/kjv/wlc/0-1/)	territory
	י	Speech: Suffix; Type: Pronominal; Person: First Person; Gender: Common; Number: Singular (https://www.blueletterbible.org/kjv/1ch/4/1/t_conc_342010/=parsing/Code:Sp1cs)	my

1 Chronicles 4:10b "If only with blessing will You continue to bless me and will You greatly increase my territory"

		SECTION:5	
		וְהָיְתָה יָדְ עִמִּי וְעָשִׂיתָ מַרְעָה לְבִלְתִּי עָצְבִּי 4:10c	

W22 וְהָיְתָה	וֹ	Strong's Number h9007; Classical Hebrew: **wāw**; Speech: conjunction https://www.blueletterbible.org/kjv/1ch/4/1/t_conc_342010/=parsing/Code:C)	and
	הָיְתָה	Classical Hebrew: **hāyâ**; Strong's Number h1961; Speech: verb; Stem: Qal; Type: Sequential Perfect (weqatal); Person: Third Person; Gender: Feminine; Number: Singular (https://www.blueletterbible.org/kjv/1ch/4/1/t_conc_342010/=parsing/Code:Vqq3fs) (https://www.blueletterbible.org/lexicon/h1961/kjv/wlc/0-1/)	may it come to pass
W23 יָדְ	יָ	Classical Hebrew: **yāḏ**; Strong's Number h3027; Speech: Noun; Type: Common; Gender: Both; Number: Singular; State: Construct (https://www.blueletterbible.org/kjv/1ch/4/1/t_conc_342010/=parsing/Code:Ncbsc) (https://www.blueletterbible.org/lexicon/h3027/kjv/wlc/0-1/)	hand
	ךָ	Speech: Suffix; Type: Pronominal; Person: Second Person; Gender: Masculine; Number: Singular (https://www.blueletterbible.org/kjv/1ch/4/1/t_conc_342010/=parsing/Code:Sp2ms) Suffix not included in Masoretic text but included in lexicon entries to make grammatical sense of the statement.	(by) Your

W24 עִמָּ עִמִּי	עִמָּ	Classical Hebrew: ʾim; Strong's Number h5973; Speech: <u>Preposition</u> (https://www.blueletterbible.org/kjv/1ch/4/1/t_conc_342010/=parsing/Code:R)	with
	י	Speech: <u>Suffix</u>; Type: <u>Pronominal</u>; Person: <u>First Person</u>; Gender: <u>Common</u>; Number: <u>Singular</u> (https://www.blueletterbible.org/kjv/1ch/4/1/t_conc_342010/=parsing/Code:Sp1cs)	me
W25 וְעָשִׂיתָ	וְ	Classical Hebrew: **wāw**; Strong's Number <u>h9007</u>; Classical Hebrew: **wāw**; Speech:<u> conjunction</u> https://www.blueletterbible.org/kjv/1ch/4/1/t_conc_342010/=parsing/Code:C)	and (that)
	עָשִׂיתָ	Classical Hebrew: ʿāśâ; Strong's Number <u>h6213</u>; Speech: <u>verb</u>; Stem: <u>Qal</u>; Type: <u>Sequential Perfect (weqatal)</u>; Person: <u>Second Person</u>; Gender: <u>Masculine</u>; Number: <u>Singular</u> (https://www.blueletterbible.org/kjv/1ch/4/1/t_conc_342010/=parsing/Code:Vqq2ms) The Biblical lexicons do not interpret this word as 'keep'. Its primary meaning is 'to do, work, make, produce.' (https://www.blueletterbible.org/lexicon/h6213/kjv/wlc/0-1/)	You will make

W26 מֵרָעָה	מִ	Strong's Number h4480; Speech: Preposition (https://www.blueletterbible.org/kjv/1ch/4/1/t conc_342010/=parsing/Code:R) See W9 above	out from
	רָעָה	Classical Hebrew: ra´; Strong's Number h7451; Speech: Noun; Type: Common; Gender: Feminine; Number: Singular; State: Absolute (https://www.blueletterbible.org/kjv/1ch/4/1/t conc_342010/=parsing/Code:Ncfsa) (https://www.blueletterbible.org/lexicon/h7451/kjv/wlc/0-1/)	this evil
W27 לְבִלְתִּי	לְ	Strong's Number h9009; Speech: Preposition (https://www.blueletterbible.org/kjv/1ch/4/1/t conc_342010/=parsing/Code:R) See W9 above	for
	בִלְתִּי	Classical Hebrew: biltî; Strong's Number h1115; Speech: Conjunction (https://www.blueletterbible.org/kjv/1ch/4/1/t conc_342010/=parsing/Code:C) (https://www.blueletterbible.org/lexicon/h1115/kjv/wlc/0-1/)	Not that (without)

W28 עָצְבְּ עָצְבִּי	עָצְבְּ	Classical Hebrew: ʿāṣaḇ; Strong's Number h6087; Speech: <u>Verb</u>; Stem: <u>Qal</u>; Type: <u>Infinitive Construct</u> (https://www.blueletterbible.org/kjv/1ch/4/1/t_conc_342010/=parsing/Code:Vqc) (https://www.blueletterbible.org/lexicon/h6087/kjv/wlc/0-1/)	pain (shaping with the way of pain)
	׳	Speech: <u>Suffix</u>; Type: <u>Pronominal</u>; Person: <u>First Person</u>; Gender: <u>Common</u>; Number: <u>Singular</u> (https://www.blueletterbible.org/kjv/1ch/4/1/t_conc_342010/=parsing/Code:Sp1cs)	me

1 Chronicles 4:10c "and may it come to pass *by* Your hand with me that You will make *me* out from this evil without shaping me with the way of pain.

SECTION:6			
4:10d וַיָּבֵא אֱלֹהִים אֵת אֲשֶׁר־שָׁאָל			
W29 וַיָּבֵא	וַ	Classical Hebrew: **wāw**; Strong's Number h9007; Speech: conjunction https://www.blueletterbible.org/kjv/1ch/4/1/t_conc_342010/=parsing/Code:C)	And
	יָבֵא	Classical Hebrew: **bô'**; Strong's Number h935; Classical Hebrew: **bô'**; Speech: verb; Stem: Hiphil; Type: Sequential imperfect (wayyiqtol); Person: Third Person; Gender: Masculine; Number: Singular (https://www.blueletterbible.org/kjv/1ch/4/1/t_conc_342010/=parsing/Code:Vqq2ms) (https://www.blueletterbible.org/lexicon/h935/kjv/wlc/0-1/)	to bring it into being
W30 אֱלֹהִים		See W15 above	Elohim (God)
W31 אֵת		Strong's Number h0853; Classical Hebrew: **'eth**; Speech: untranslated particle (http://lexiconcordance.com/hebrew/0853.html) See W21 above	(granted)

W32 אֲשֶׁר־ שָׁאַל	אֲשֶׁר־	Strong's Number h834; Classical Hebrew: **'ăšer**; Speech: <u>verb</u>; Speech: <u>Participle</u>; Type: <u>Relative</u> (https://www.blueletterbible.org/kjv/1ch/4/1/t_conc_342010/=parsing/Code:Tr) (https://www.blueletterbible.org/lexicon/h834/kjv/wlc/0-1/)	that which
	שָׁאַל	Strong's Number h7592; Classical Hebrew: **šā'al'**; Speech: <u>verb</u>; Stem: <u>Qal</u>; Type: <u>Perfect (qatal)</u>; Person: <u>Third Person</u>; Gender: <u>Masculine</u>; Number: <u>Singular</u> (https://www.blueletterbible.org/kjv/1ch/4/1/t_conc_342010/=parsing/Code:Vqp3ms) (https://www.blueletterbible.org/lexicon/h7592/kjv/wlc/0-1)	he asked for

1 Chronicles 4:10d "And to bring it into being Elohim (God) *granted* that which he asked for."

BIBLIOGRAPHY

Bible Versions used:

Scripture quotations marked New International Version (NIV) are taken from - THE HOLY BIBLE, NEW INTERNATIONAL VERSION®, NIV® Copyright © 1973, 1978, 1984, 2011 by Biblica, Inc.® Used by permission. All rights reserved worldwide.

Scripture quotations marked New American Standard Bible (NASB) are taken from - New American Standard Bible®, Copyright © 1960, 1971, 1977, 1995, 2020 by The Lockman Foundation. All rights reserved.

Scripture quotations marked New King James Version (NKJV) are taken from - New King James Version®. Copyright © 1982 by Thomas Nelson. Used by permission. All rights reserved.

Scripture quotations marked New Living Translation (NLT) are taken from - *Holy Bible,* New Living Translation, copyright © 1996, 2004, 2015 by Tyndale House Foundation. Used by permission of Tyndale House Publishers, Inc., Carol Stream, Illinois 60188. All rights reserved.

Scripture quotations marked Living Bible (TLB) are taken from - The Living Bible copyright © 1971 by Tyndale House Foundation. Used

All Scripture marked with the designation "GW" is taken from GOD'S WORD®. © 1995, 2003, 2013, 2014, 2019, 2020 by God's Word to the Nations Mission Society. Used by permission.

Scripture quotations marked Blue Letter Bible (BLB) are taken from - (n.d.). Blue Letter Bible. https://www.blueletterbible.org/

Scripture quotations marked The Passion Translation (TPT) are taken from - The Passion Translation®. Copyright © 2017, 2018, 2020 by Passion & Fire Ministries, Inc. Used by permission. All rights reserved. https://www.thepassiontranslation.com/

Scripture quotations marked J.B. Phillips New Testament (PHILLIPS) are taken from - The New Testament in Modern English by J.B Phillips copyright © 1960, 1972 J. B. Phillips. Administered by The Archbishops' Council of the Church of England. Used by Permission.

Other References:

The Prayer of Jabez: A Valley Bible Church Position Paper www.valleybible.net Completed: January 2001. Retrieved from: https://www.csmedia1.com/valleybible.net/jabez.pdf December 13, 2020

Jeff A. Benner, Learn the Ancient Pictographic Hebrew Script, Retrieved from: https://www.ancient-hebrew.org/learn/learn-the-ancient-pictographic-hebrew-script.htm#aleph January 27, 2023

Prof. Brian Tice, B.Sci., M.Sci. Day 5: The Biblical Meaning of "Blessing". Retrieved from: https://adiakrisis.wordpress.com/biblical-studies-articles/hebraic-observations-on-the-creation-narrative-genesis-11-23/day-5-the-biblical-meaning-of-blessing/ April 4, 2017

R. Christopher Heard, Echoes of Genesis in 1 Chronicles 4:9–10: An Intertextual and Contextual Reading of Jabez's Prayer DOI: https://doi.org/10.5508/jhs.2002.v4.a2 Retrieved from: https://jhsonline.org/index.php/jhs/article/view/5859 Dec 12, 2022

Emil G. Hirsch, Kaufmann Kohler, JABEZ: Retrieved from: https://www.jewishencyclopedia.com/articles/8369-jabez December 14, 2022

Benjamin Shaw, ThM, PhD (candidate), The Prayer of Jabez: A Biblical-Theological Examination, 26 Feb 2003. Retrieved from: https://chalcedon.edu/resources/articles/the-prayer-of-jabez-a-biblical-theological-examination, May 1, 2017

Skip Moen, Ph.D., The Real Prayer of Jabez, April 11, 2021. Retrieved from: https://skipmoen.com/2021/04/the-real-prayer-of-jabez/, January 18, 2023

Strong, James. The New Strong's Exhaustive Concordance of the Bible. Nashville: T. Nelson, 1990.

Wilkinson, B., Kopp, D., & Dudash, C. M. (2000). The prayer of Jabez: breaking through to the blessed life. Sisters, Or., Multnomah.

BIOGRAPH

My own journey, while not told in this account, reflects the reality of the truths these pages contain. I grew up on a farm, left school at 15, never completing high school and having no formal academic or trade qualifications. I am not gifted in some extraordinary way so from the natural standpoint this book should never have been written. But the relentless pursuit to push beyond the boundaries and confines of life's circumstances has led to this adventure and this outcome.

It is my deep desire to live a life that counts for something beyond my mere existence and through these pages I want to inspire you to do the same and to live **'Beyond Ordinary'.**

www.ingramcontent.com/pod-product-compliance
Lightning Source LLC
LaVergne TN
LVHW051132080426
835510LV00018B/2368